Praise for
the Art of resilience

"When life gets out of control, be sure to have this book handy. Carol Orsborn's thought-provoking stories remind us that life is a surprising spiral full of both delight and disappointment. By practicing the art of resilience, you will learn to bounce back and rejoice in the divine adventure of life."

—Salli Rasberry,
author of *Living Your Life Out Loud:
How to Unlock Your Creativity and Unleash Your Joy*

"A wonderful new book about remembering the most important thing in life—love."

—Gerald G. Jampolsky, M.D.,
author of *Love Is Letting Go of Fear*

"Carol Orsborn has written a wonderful book to help people not only survive, but thrive, after disappointments. An extraordinary guide to help you bounce back and get on track! Read it today. You won't be disappointed."

—Richard Carlson, Ph.D.,
author of *Don't Sweat the Small Stuff*

the *A*rt of

resilience

Also by

CAROL ORSBORN

ENOUGH IS ENOUGH
Simple Solutions for Complex People

HOW WOULD CONFUCIUS ASK FOR A RAISE?
One Hundred Enlightened Solutions for Tough Business Problems

SOLVED BY SUNSET
The Right-Brain Way to Resolve Whatever's Bothering You
in One Day or Less

the Art of resilience

100 PATHS TO WISDOM AND STRENGTH IN AN UNCERTAIN WORLD

CAROL ORSBORN

Three Rivers Press / New York

Author's Note

*Participants in the Inner Excellence Roundtable and
clients of the Dan Orsborn Company have contributed case
histories and anecdotal support for the principles shared in this
book. When requested, I have honored their desire for
anonymity by changing personal and company
names and fictionalizing details.*

Published by Three Rivers Press, a division of Crown Publishers, Inc., 201 East 50th Street, New York, New York 10022. Member of the Crown Publishing Group.

Random House, Inc. New York, Toronto, London, Sydney, Auckland

http://www.randomhouse.com/

Three Rivers Press and colophon are trademarks of Crown Publishers, Inc.

Printed in the United States of America

Design by Lynne Amft

Library of Congress Cataloging-in-Publication Data

is available upon request.

ISBN 0-609-80061-2

10 9 8 7 6 5 4

*With great affection, I dedicate this book to
my father and mother, Lloyd and Mae Matzkin,
for teaching me to take my greatest joy from the simple gifts of life:
music, love, and laughter.*

Acknowledgments

I thank my agent, Patti Breitman, for providing my writing career with a loving center, and my editor, Shaye Areheart, for giving wings to my stories.

Thanks, too, to all of the people at Harmony and Crown Books, whose passion for their work expresses itself in every detail. In particular, my gratitude goes to Leslie Meredith, Patty Eddy, Amy Zelvin, Dina Siciliano, and Mary Schuck.

As always, I acknowledge my family—my husband, Dan; my daughter, Jody; and my son, Grant. Thank you, Grant, for your inspired in-house editing!

Finally, thank you to my professors at Vanderbilt University Divinity School and to all the many writers, mystics, and teachers credited in the pages of this book. Through you, I have become part of a rich spiritual community including individuals from many centuries, continents, and religious traditions. May this book honor the gifts of wisdom and knowledge you have shared with me over the years.

Contents

Introduction   1
Preface   7

Stage I: Point of Impact
1. Keep Breathing   11
2. Seek Refuge   13
3. Light a Crying Candle   15
4. Take Turns   17
5. Let Go   20
6. Write a Letter Expressing Your Anger   22
7. Experience Pain as Purification   24
8. Call Your Friends and Listen   26
9. You Don't Weep Alone   27
10. Direct Your Complaints Upward   30
11. Envision the Best Possible Outcome, Too   33
12. Exercise Your Spirit   36

Stage II: Time to Regroup
13. Change Only What You Must   41
14. Take an Emotional Vacation   43
15. Let Your Yearning Grow Larger Than Your Fear   46
16. Ask Your Pain for Answers   48
17. There Is Always Something You Can Do   51
18. Listen for the Lyrics   53
19. Rerun the Upset, Imagining Everyone
    Involved to Be Four Years Old   55
20. Clean Up Your Address Book   58
21. Take a Notebook to a Cafe and Write the
    Story of Your Life   61

Stage III: Signs of Spring
22. Model Your Life on the Spiral, Not the Stick   67
23. Give Yourself Roses in Winter   70

24. Do Something You Loved as a Child   72

25. Solve Something   74

26. Treat Yourself as You Would a Best Friend   77

27. Find Something for Which You Can Feel
    Grateful   79

28. Tell Your Story to Someone Who Will
    Listen Quietly   82

29. If You Picked the Wrong Person to Talk To . . . 84

30. Break a Sweat   85

31. Put Yourself Back in the Center of Your Life   86

32. Create Your Own Calendar of Holidays   87

33. Set Miracles in Motion   89

34. Let the Embers Catch Fire   91

Stage IV: The Authentic Life

35. Keep Things Simple   95

36. Read Unauthorized Biographies   97

37. Are You Willing to Pay the Rent?   100

38. Indulge Your Emotions   103

39. Think About Somebody Else's Problems   106

40. Entertain the Kindness of Strangers   108

41. Consider the Consequences   110

42. Tell the Whole Truth   113

43. Get Used to Dust   114

44. Trade in Your Sack of Troubles   116

Stage V: Unfinished Business

45. Value the Unexpected   121

46. Eat Your Mistake   123

47. Deal With It   125

48. Confess Your Shortcomings to an
    Empty Shower Stall   129

49. Spend Quality Time With Someone
    Worse Off Than You   132

50. All You Can Do   134

51. Counteract Your Tendencies 136
52. Ride a Roller Coaster 138
53. Laugh Into the Mirror 139
54. Bless Their Hearts 142
55. Remember That You Are Loved 144
56. Build Anew 147

Stage VI: Uncharted Territory

57. Set Sail for Open Waters 151
58. Go Wild 154
59. Try to Stop the Waves From Rolling In 157
60. Escape From a Chinese Finger Puzzle 160
61. Color Outside the Lines 162
62. Pray as You Are 164
63. Ask the Big Questions 166
64. Give Up Needing to Know 167
65. Withhold Judgment 169
66. Hold a Garage Sale 171
67. Let Your Curiosity Lend You Courage 173

Stage VII: Sacred Space

68. Place Your Wager on Meaning 179
69. Dip Your Toes in Mystic Waters 182
70. Pull in Your Oars 185
71. Provide Shade 189
72. Think of Yourself as Experientially Gifted 191
73. Sit Alone in a Sacred Place 193
74. Trust the Impulse to Pray More Than the Prayer Itself 194
75. Choose Your Wishes Wisely 196
76. Wake Up Singing 198
77. Watch the Sun Rise 201

Stage VIII: A New Center

78. Go Fishing 205
79. Grab Your Flashlight 208
80. You Never Awaken to the Same Day Twice 212
81. Take a Stand 214
82. The Better Question Is Not How to Become Happy, but Rather What Is Being Asked of You 217
83. Wrestle With Angels 219

Stage IX: Higher-Quality Problems

84. Seek a Shaman 225
85. Clean Up the Mess 229
86. Choose Problems That Are Worthy of You 231
87. Make a Two-Hundred-Year Plan 233
88. Blaze a Secret Route 236
89. Be Specialized—Not Special 238
90. Do Your Utmost 241

Stage X: Beyond Resilience

91. Allow Yourself to Be Changed 245
92. Carve Something Out of Wood 247
93. Teach the Lump in Your Throat to Sing 249
94. Skate On 252
95. Set Your Dry Bones Dancing 254
96. Jump at the Sun 257
97. Find Someone to Tickle You 258
98. Cultivate a Taste for the Bittersweet 259
99. Try Again 261
100. Make Your Life a Work of Art 263

The Ten Stages of Resilience 265
Sources 271

You can't always stop bad things from happening to you. But remember, you can't stop the good things from happening to you, either—often when you're least expecting them.

the Art of
resilience

Introduction

*"Life moves upward and lets the mistakes sink
down behind it."*

—THE *I* CHING

Three thousand years ago, the ancient Chinese understood that
every aspect of life is in a constant state of change. At any given
moment, certain aspects of our lives are falling away—and certain
aspects are birthing. So it is that we progress through our days,
leaving behind qualities and aspects that no longer serve us and ac-
quiring new depths of awareness about who we are becoming.

More often than not, pain is the catalyst that causes us to shed
outmoded ways of being and to stumble with various combina-
tions of grace and muttering onto the threshold of new passions.
The ancient Chinese sought to master the art of resilience by accepting, rather than fearing, change as the way of the world. As we
approach the turn of the millennium, we have access to the knowledge and wisdom of not only these ancient seekers, but of the mystics, philosophers, and scientists of virtually every era and culture.
From Christian mystics to Hasidic rabbis, from Sufi masters to scientists, this book is inspired by these spiritually gifted individuals
who teach us through many symbolic, philosophical, and even scientific symbols the core truth of universal faith: that there is a tendency for good to prevail. Call it Tao, Life Force, Great Spirit,

Energy, or God. Or, as Nobel prize–winning chemist Ilya Prigogine postulated, call it the theory of dissipative structures. Utilizing the scientific method, Prigogine theorized that people, things, and events are involved in a continuous exchange of energy, impacting one another on an ongoing basis. When something disturbs or upsets the system, the components have the capacity to reorganize themselves into a higher order. The new order tends to move away from destructive propensities and toward actions and states representing a greater capability to protect the system from threats in the future.

We do not stand alone, rigid objects in a static world. Rather, we are part of the complex interplay of the entire energy field, both internal and external. Change any part of it, physical or metaphysical, and you impact the whole. This book is based on the premise that you have it within your power to effect a response that will bring forth from the things that happen to you the greatest good possible. This is not to say that there are not certain times when crises may overwhelm your ability to recover on your own. If you have a suspicion that this may be the case for you, I urge you to seek professional help. But understand that even this act, the recognition that you need assistance, sets in motion forces leading to recovery.

The summer that birthed the idea for this book gave me many opportunities to practice the art of resilience. In a short period of time, I faced challenges, pain, and disappointment in my career and personal relationships as well as physical well-being.

My initial response to my troubles echoed an incident that pastor Bruce Larson tells in his book *Living Beyond Our Fears: Discovering Life When You're Scared to Death.* Bruce shares the story of an elderly friend of his, who had decided to invest all of his retirement money in the stock market. Then came the crash of October 1987. His friend's entire life savings were wiped out in one fell swoop. Bruce called his friend and asked how he was doing.

"I'm sleeping like a baby," his friend replied.

"I wake up every three or four hours and cry."

Ironically, crisis is not built into the fabric of the actual events our lives deliver to us. Rather, psychologists contend that crisis occurs "when our theories about ourselves in relation to the outside world go fundamentally wrong," explains author Glenys Parry: "It is as if your front door, one day, instead of opening when you turned the key, gave you an electric shock."

It is the dissonance between our expectations and our outcomes that causes the pain—not the outcomes alone. Foremost among our expectations is our belief that pain is something to be avoided at all costs; that it is bad for you. Suffering does not fit our theory about what it takes to succeed in life and so we fail to concede that pain is inevitable in each of our lives. The fact that each of us suffers misfortunes from time to time may be our society's darkest, deepest secret. From a quick survey of the self-help spiritual supermarket, it is apparent that as a whole, we would rather focus on the abundance of the universe. On prosperity. Thinking positively, we work to build life structures so big and powerful that it would take an army tank of a disappointment to break through. If even so, upset threatens to break through, we'll try another strategy. We'll simplify ourselves to the point where there's nothing left to lose; we'll get busy so that we won't have time to feel our losses; or we'll medicate the pain with drugs, alcohol, or food. Perhaps that is why sales of Prozac are so high—and why most of the gurus on the talk-show circuits place their emphasis on mastering success to avoid pain rather than on how to deal with and rebound from it when it occurs. As a result, we know a great deal about how to push through our fears and feelings to attempt to achieve our goals, but we know precious little about how to suffer gracefully and productively when we are up against forces we cannot control.

While our culture tends to call surrendering to pain "apathy," the truth is that the Greek root for the word *apathy* actually means the avoidance, not the experience, of suffering. It is not when you are feeling the pain of setbacks that you are being apathetic, but rather, when you squash your fear of appearing morbid, stupid, guilty, faithless, emotional, or powerless. Suffering pain fully and wholly is not a passive act of resignation. Rather, it is the dynamic groundwork from which, lovingly tended, the seeds of transformation and transcendence will sprout.

Contemporary psychologists and theologians are just now shaping theories of recovery that the wisest of our ancient philosophers and mystics intuited to be true thousands of years ago. There are stages to the process of recovery, stages that you will be encouraged to traverse through the pages of this book. The process is initiated the moment you recognize that it is not only the actuality of the challenge you face that has caused you to search deeper for answers, but that the real issue is that the presenting event has outstripped your current capacity to manage the world to your satisfaction. You can't be good enough, try hard enough, be smart enough, meditate enough, eat enough vegetarian meals, and say enough prayers to get your life to turn out the way you'd like each and every time. Certainly, you can influence your destiny by utilizing all the spiritual, physical, emotional, and practical technology your spirit can muster—but you cannot guarantee any single one of your outcomes. You cannot even know for sure what will happen to you one second from now.

You may struggle to hold on to the things that you thought you could count on—like branches hanging over the quagmire of hopelessness that threatens to take you under. And then the branches crack. Destiny swallows you deeply into the mystery. Let it. For this is the very route to meaning. To extract this meaning, your life must seek to find the powerful fulcrum point where there exists balance between opposites. On one hand, there are times when you will feel the vital drive of hope, ambition, and dreams enticing you forward. On the other hand, there are times when the finitude of the human condition presses in upon you. Surrender, and you will gain velocity and direction from your limitations. The philosopher Rollo May guided us to think of our lives as water flowing to the sea. Without its banks, there can be no river. Without your disappointments, your duties and responsibilities pressing against your dreams, giving shape and direction to your destiny, you could never reach the sea.

By distilling and applying the wisdom of those who came before me to my own recovery, I recognized why it is that the art of resilience depends so heartily on the principle of surrendering rather than pushing through. For it is when we loosen our grip on reality that disappointment has the opportunity to reorganize our understandings of ourselves and the world into a higher order. Writer Dorothy Lessing notes:

Almost all men . . . have strange imaginings. The strangest of these is a belief that they can progress only by improvement. Those who understand will realize that we are much more in need of stripping off than adding on.

As I write this, four months after the last of my summer's disappointments, I find my pain to have gently receded. In its place is a mysteriously replenished supply of faith. It is not that all of the issues that caused me pain this summer have been rectified, but that somehow, my spirit has grown large enough to encompass a broader spectrum of the human condition. I feel blessed to have this opportunity to share what I have learned about the art of resilience with you.

Preface

You have encountered obstacles in your journey through life. Perhaps the pain you feel has to do with a relationship that is important to you, a change in your job or financial situation, or worrisome news about your health. At this moment, you may feel alone with your wounds. Outwardly, you may feel resentment about others who participated in your suffering—or about the untrustworthiness of the world. Secretly, you may harbor shame about the role you played. Swirling around it all is a sense of having lost your footing. The ground you thought—or at least hoped—you could count on feels as though it were crumbling beneath your feet.

But the truth is, there is nothing that fate has brought you that you can't handle. Your recovery will occur sooner or later. You will feel yourself again—and this time, your self will be standing on the firmer ground of experience hard won through today's suffering.

There is one difference between those individuals who rebound sooner and those who rebound later from the disappointments they've suffered. Those who rebound sooner have opened their hearts to the notion that resilience is an art that can be learned. When misfortune comes their way, they do not let their pain whip them into extremes—neither frenzy nor denial. Rather, they engage with their pain, trusting that however complete the wreckage, the greatest possible good can yet emerge.

To become a candidate for mastery, you do not need to feel grateful for what has happened to you. Resilience can be acquired whether you are feeling sad, angry, depressed, or numb. You don't even need to have faith that this will work for you. For the time being, if you are feeling depleted, these pages will hold the faith for you.

The subsequent ten stages will acquaint you with the art of resilience. They are organized in a progression, from the initial shock of impact, through both short- and long-term stages of recovery. The words have been inspired by those who have overcome setbacks in their lives and careers. These are the voices of those who have spoken to me from the pages of books, in the classrooms I frequent both as a student and as a teacher, and through both the chance encounter and the most intimate connections that grace my life. These are spirits whose lives have revealed to me the innermost secret of resilience: The deeper the channels pain carves into your soul, the greater the capacity for joy your soul can contain. Mastering the art of resilience does much more than restore you to who you once thought you were. Rather, you emerge from the experience transformed into a truer expression of who you are really meant to be.

Prepare to be surprised.

Point of Impact

"There is only one thing I dread:
not to be worthy of my sufferings."

—Fyodor Dostoyevsky

In the beginning, the pain is acute. Your tendency is to pull back—to avoid the suffering at all costs. But the emotions you are experiencing are not the obstacles to your healing. In fact, they are the very means of your deliverance. Your tears will wash away the illusions of what you once believed to be true. You may confront loss, humiliation, powerlessness, uncertainty, mortality. But you cannot rebuild a life structure stronger than it was, unless these bricks of the human condition, too, are laid into the foundation. At this point of your journey, the best thing to do is learn to be patient with your pain. As you do, you will discover that without having to do anything but feel, you are doing the important work of providing the basis upon which a more authentic existence can be built.

1

Keep Breathing

*"Pain can make a whole winter bright, like fever,
force us to live deep and hard . . ."*

—MAY SARTON

Something happened. Right now, at the moment of impact, the pain is uniquely yours. You may have been in this place before—or you may have marshaled your forces to keep this moment at bay for years. Whichever the case, the very thought that you could keep things under control now carries the capacity to wound. You worked hard, you planned, you strategized, you did your best. And yet, here you stand, your dream strewn about you like so many pieces of a broken vessel.

Sorrow seeps through the ceramic cracks, mixed with your tears. As the once-solid ground, moistened by pain, turns to mud beneath your feet, the old wounds of a lifetime unexpectedly surface as shards of broken vessels past. You try to rouse yourself from the sinkhole that is swallowing your world, but a dank lethargy settles upon you, thick and heavy. The pain, like fever, sweeps over you.

Then come the questions. *How quickly must I respond? How far will I sink? What did I do? What must I do? Will I ever be okay again? Will I survive? Should I feel ashamed? Why did this happen to me?*

The *I Ching*, the book that contains the wisdom of ancient China, cries out to you: "A hundred thousand times you lose your treasures. Do not go in pursuit of them. After seven days, you will get them back again." Three thousand years of resilience asks you to trust that there will be a time for you to act. A time for you to answer the questions that press down upon you. There will be a time soon when you will know what to do.

Meanwhile, keep breathing. As you breathe in, breathe in life and light and the promise of healing. Breathe out. Breathe out the pain. Breathe slowly and deeply, trusting that the same life force that keeps the process of renewal alive in your body is fueling the urge to heal. Your breath, the beating of your heart, are already carrying you forward toward recovery. Even as you seek refuge from the fever of pain that shudders through you, your spirit is burning away the darkness.

2

Seek Refuge

No matter how deep the wound, there is a place you can curl up inside that embraces you just as you are. Where is it that you feel the urge to be right now? The easy chair in your living room, the bench by the pond, the hand-knit sweater two sizes too big? Everybody needs a place they can go to rest, sheltered from the past and the future. A place where you can live one moment at a time. If you can't physically go to this place, find something that reminds you of it. A photograph. A fire in the fireplace. A hand-carried stone.

Where can you go where you will be taken exactly as you are? Nothing added on or taken away. Embracing you within the familiarity of their textures, fragrances, and curves, your favorite places and things, accepting you here, now, without judgment. Whether your place is by the side of a pond or sheltered beneath the covers of your bed, wherever you are, wherever you go, you are suspended in the only present you can touch, hear, and smell.

When I suffer misfortune, I carry my wounded spirit to Radnor Lake. Cousin to Walden Pond, Radnor's bark trails wind through timeless woods populated by owls, rabbits, and squirrels. Whether I come to Radnor from triumph or from despair, whether I experience my life to be populated by people who love me or by no one, the lake recognizes me only as one of its own. I sit on my favorite wooden bench, set so close to the edge of the water, I imagine that I am on a raft adrift in the middle of the sea. Ducks swim by, their feet noisily kicking concentric circles into the water. Nobody stops to pay any attention to my misfortune here. Leaves rustle and I turn just in time to see the bushy tail of a rabbit diving into the brush.

I have been here so many times, celebrating the simple joys that fill my life. This time, the world I have left behind—including the rippling effects of problems that I fear will be waiting for me when I return home—is filled with the memory of pain. And yet I have the supreme privilege of having this place to come, to be, no matter what. Same ducks. Same ripples. I touch my hands to my face. On some deep, deep level, the present moment can be counted upon to bear witness to the eternal. I am still here. Where I am, many things are yet possible.

3

Light a Crying Candle

"Tears are not the pain. They are the healing."

—Dr. Annette Goodheart

Light a candle and stay with it until the last flame flickers out. If you have suffered but a minor annoyance, you may find a left-over birthday candle to be just the right size. If you have suffered a great blow, you may need to seek out a large candle that will burn for many, many hours. Perhaps you will need a candle so big, you will need to light it every night for a week or a month or even a year or more. As the candle burns, you are asked to do only one thing. Feel.

Grief, anger, sadness, shame, embarrassment, fear.

Emotions will leap at you from the burning wick, but watch out. Nipping hungrily at the heart of the flame's blue palette will be an orange lick, chiding you for sitting still in your puddle of feelings instead of swinging into action. *You ought to be implementing some plan for recovery. Weighing the possibilities. Making amends or taking retribution.* But resilience cannot be birthed through busy little projects. Of course you would like to get on with things as quickly as possible. Buttress your life structure over again, throw up the scaffolding, plaster the cracks. As the blue-and-orange flame licks at the melting wax, a hundred times, you tell yourself you've indulged your anger and your grief long enough. *Shake it off and get on with it already.*

But the emotions you are experiencing are not your obstacles to recovery. Don't you see? At this, the point of impact, they are the very means of your deliverance. Only your tears contain sufficient power to tear down the battered remains of the structures that could not hold their own against what has happened. Be grateful for your tears of anger and grief, which keep you from rising too quickly to the occasion. Rather, mired in the straw and mud of true emotion, you confront loss, humiliation, powerlessness, uncertainty, mortality. You cannot rebuild the old structure stronger than it was, unless these bricks, too, are laid into the foundation. Leave any one of these out, and you will sway precariously to and fro with every breeze that blows. But build your life structure upon the truth of the human condition, and you will withstand anything that fate sends its way.

4

Take Turns

Recently, I had coffee with an old friend. Every year for decades, she had met with five of her best high-school buddies for an annual retreat of friendship and reflection. I asked how things had gone.

"It was emotionally exhausting," she said, sighing loudly.

"Did things come up for you to deal with?" I asked.

"No. Things came up for my friends. All at the same time. And I was the only one who knew what to do."

"What do you mean?"

"When I was younger, my life fell apart. My husband and I split. I had no job training, and I had to figure out a way to support my young children. My friends were all settled in with cushy situations, so they could really be there for me. There was a decade

17

or so when I guess you could call me their charity project. They saw me through my educational program, starting a little secretarial service, parenting issues, and getting back on track emotionally. I never did remarry, but somehow—with their love and support—I put together a great network of friends who function as my family. The kids grew up fine—my friends came to every one of their graduations and special events. And the little secretarial service I started grew into one of the biggest in the city. I'm doing great."

"So why are you exhausted?"

"They all hit midlife crisis at the same time, never having had to deal with much of anything. They thought they were getting an easy ride this lifetime. But something's spun out of control for each one of them. Laura's husband walked out on her for his assistant. Marlene's son is on drugs and dropped out of college. March has been diagnosed with breast cancer, and so on and so on. The sad thing is that they have so few skills to deal with troublesome matters. In fact, they weren't even using the few skills they had because they were so busy trying to wrestle their illusions back in place.

"Turns out that because of what happened to me, I'm the only one who isn't terrified of life. I've been tested and I know I'm a survivor. They really don't know the same about themselves yet. Luckily, I'm strong enough to be able to give back to them the gift of love they bestowed on me when I needed it. To tell you the truth, it feels good being able to give to them, knowing that there are emotional places that I've already progressed through in my life that I'll never have to go back to again. It's not that I won't be sad or have unlucky breaks. But I'm not afraid of pain anymore because I know

now that the place where you have been broken is the very place that heals back strongest."

The healing process begins here, now. If you are patient with your pain, you will discover that without having to do anything but feel, you strengthen the foundation of your soul upon which a more authentic existence will be built.

Let Go

$\mathcal{T}$here are times when the things that have happened are so painful, you quite simply cannot grasp why they have happened to you and those you care about. At such moments, your mind cannot help you. Your heart, too, may be frozen in fear. And yet, even as you cling rigid and cold with fright to the last remnants of what used to be, destiny has pushed you off the cliff. Careening into the void, you find yourself clutching at dark air.

Surely, in such a state, you cannot be expected to operate powerfully. Chances are you are unable to operate at all. In the endless void, only one course of action remains: to let go. To unclench your fists and throw yourself into the swirling dark currents, arms and legs outstretched, seeing where it takes you. *Where the mystery takes you.*

You cry out for answers and the infinite whispers to you: *Float helplessly on my black tides with only the faintest hope that all is not lost.*

Very soon, you will see your fate not as dark tides in the void, but as loving hands gently guiding you home.

6

Write a Letter
Expressing Your Anger

Write the letter, then put it away for a week before deciding whether to send, save, or burn it. Say exactly how it is that you feel to whoever you feel most deserves to bear the brunt of your feelings. You have, after all, the right to be angry.

We spend so much time in our society improving ourselves, thinking positively, being upbeat, that we seldom give ourselves the opportunity to give vent to something fundamental to us all: Life isn't fair. This is true for you. This is true for everybody. It isn't fair that good people suffer needlessly, nor that bad people progress when they should be punished. It's something worth being angry about.

The other day, I passed beneath an underpass on the way to

taking care of an unpleasant task. Across it, someone had scrawled the spray-painted words "There is no such thing as gravity. The earth sucks."

So you are angry about your misfortune. You are angry at others who played a part. Or you are angry at those who failed to intervene. You are angry at yourself for getting into this mess. Or you are angry at the universe for failing to protect you from this pain. You won't be in bad company if this is how you feel. The Christian mystic Teresa of Avila once prayed, "I do not wonder, God, that you have so few friends, from the way you treat them."

Write it all down. Pour your emotion onto your paper, understanding this. The degree of anger you feel for what is unjust is directly proportional to your capacity to generate passion for how you'd like things to be. There will be a time when you will be grateful at your great potential to bestir yourself to action.

7

Experience Pain as Purification

What if you were to experience the pain you are feeling not as damaging you—but as purifying you?

Shame and guilt, when held as purification, can burn off old ways of being. As the heat of regret flows through your body, visualize the flames devouring the pain you have caused others and yourself.

When sacrificed on the altar of faith, anger can transform into compassion. Fear into peace.

Perhaps your pain is physical. Experience the discomfort as purification of your spirit. You can begin by identifying the most dominant quality in your life you no longer want or need. For instance, perhaps you are no longer willing to let other people push you around. Or maybe you are tired of driving yourself so hard. As you experience the pain, visualize it burning off aspects of yourself that you are ready to release.

The first time I transformed pain into purification was at the dentist's office. I am not brave about my teeth. And now, suddenly, after a lifetime of being able to count on my teeth to hold a steady course, there seems to be a crown a year. For the dentist, crowns are just another day's work. But for me, the busy fingers at work in mysterious reaches of my mouth whittle away not only at old metals, but at my understanding of myself. Other people have crowns—not someone of my age and vitality.

I try to gurgle out my protest, but the dentist tells me to open wider, please. And then, suddenly, blessedly, my mind seizes on something big enough to keep me occupied. Who was I, after all, to believe that I was specially selected by fate never to have to go through what all those who came before me endured? No matter how vivid my memories of childhood, I, too, was destined to age. Empathy floods into me, as I realize how much negative judgment I'd heaped on those I deemed somehow less blessed than myself. Like pinecones caught in a forest fire, the hard shells of my naive arrogance crack and pop, revealing the first signs of a humble acceptance of the inevitability of aging and the tenderest seed of compassion for the human condition.

The greater the pain, the greater the purification. As discomfort burns out that which you no longer want or need in your life, imagine healthy young seeds of new, desirable qualities taking root. The ash of broken dreams past, watered by your tears, will enrich the soil from which the new growth will emerge.

8

Call Your Friends and Listen

Long ago, in a small Chinese village, a young woman suffered a great loss. Her son had been taken by illness, leaving her in despair. She went to see Buddha, telling him of her tragedy. The Buddha could do miracles, and so she asked him to restore her child to her.

The Buddha agreed to do this—but only if she could bring to him a single grain of mustard from any home in the village where no one had ever felt the pain of such a loss.

The young woman set out immediately. But at every door, she was met by someone whose sufferings had been as great as her own. She could not collect even a single grain of mustard. As she left the final portal, she achieved enlightenment. She returned to the Buddha, to express her boundless gratitude. At last, she was able to lay her son's spirit to rest.

9

You Don't Weep Alone

When your family and friends tell you that you were sent this painful situation as a lesson, that it is your karma, a gift, or even punishment, they are trying to be helpful. By putting you into the loop—proposing that you did something that merited the universe's special attention—the assumption is that you can now do something to fix the situation. Do better, think more positively, cleanse your spirit, and the universe will make sure this doesn't happen to you again.

Of course, it is true that we can learn from the things that happen to us. Often, we can even come to recognize that something good has come out of situations we would rather have avoided. When the misfortunes that befall me are not so great, I can often find the meaning in them even as I cry painful tears. It is possible, then, to think of life as having sent me these challenges in order to train or test me for some greater purpose. I can think of my problems at these times as a lesson or a gift.

Sometimes, I can even accept the pain as punishment. I experience a power greater than myself as a caring parent sending me misfortune as tough love.

But there are other times when the pain is so great, so seemingly arbitrarily executed, I cannot believe that the universe would choose this particular way to show that love. To call many of the things that happen to us "gifts" is to trivialize and degrade both ourselves and the divine. At these times in particular, you must stay alert in order to confront the real question underlying your friends' attempts to be helpful: *Is the divine really the source of your pain? Is God the sender of holocaust and cruelty and evil?*

This I heartily reject. If you cannot speak of lessons and gifts before a starving child in Rwanda, or the innocent victim of a drive-by shooting in Los Angeles, then you should not unthinkingly apply this notion of the divine to yourself and your situation, either. At these times, you must have the courage to confront the possibility that what happened to you or to others contains no inherently useful meaning whatsoever. Sometimes the only lesson to be gleaned is that life brings with it no guarantees. Things don't always make sense. They are not always deserved. In the end, all we can know for certain is the mystery.

If what happened to you is not a lesson, gift, or punishment, with what, then, are you left? How are you to experience meaning in the midst of your suffering?

In the darkest hours of the Warsaw ghetto, as Jewish families witnessed the destruction of their world, a rabbi shared words of comfort with those who turned to him with questions of meaning.

"You can weep over your suffering until you despair, or you can feel in your weeping that God weeps along with you."

This is my God. Not God who is the source of my suffering. But rather, God who shares the burden of my sorrow and who promises me that never need I suffer alone.

10

Direct Your Complaints Upward

Your jagged-edged complaints are cycling through your brain over and over again in an endless loop.

I'm sunk. This time, I've really gotten in over my head. I'm sick and tired of feeling so much pain. I'm so alone. The whole world is against me. I've got nowhere to turn. I'm so ashamed.

Because the words seem so justified, you hang on to them. Your endless muttering is all that's left of the reality you once thought you could count on. So you hang on to their monotonous litany.

But if left undisciplined, the dark-hued words will trap your pain in your mind, where they can do no good. Perhaps it is time to consider the possibility that your grievances could have somewhere to go where they could get things moving again.

Where is this place? Send them to the heart of the universe, where anything is possible.

Here's how. This time, as you witness the droning words of complaint looping through your mind, simply insert your name for the divine periodically. For practice, go ahead and fill in the blanks.

_____, *I'm sunk. This time, I've really gotten in over my head. I'm sick and tired of feeling so much pain.* _____, *I'm so alone. The whole world is against me. I've got nowhere to turn.* _____, *I'm so ashamed.*

By addressing your grievances to a power greater than yourself, you make your complaints potent. Tempered by divine compassion, the sharp edges of pain round and soften. Infinite grievance turns into infinite compassion. Your complaints will now empower rather than deplete you.

Oddly enough, you don't have to believe that this works for it to be effective. You don't need to know that there's a divine healing power standing by to respond to your entreaties. In fact, you can be cynical, angry, despondent, abandoned, or resentful.

You don't even have to be worthy for it to work. In fact, there is a rich mystical tradition that contends that it is your very awareness of your undeservedness that makes your prayer effective. Thankfully, we need not feel particularly effective or powerful in our own right to be considered a candidate for the in-breaking of spirit. Throughout the texts of many faith traditions, it is often the unlikeliest candidates who are afforded this opportunity. A sheepherder, stuttering on a mountaintop. A beggarwoman, reaching out secretly to touch a sacred hem. As Rabbi Abraham Joshua Heschel related, the proper way to present one's self in prayer is full of fear and trembling at our presumption for being the flawed human beings we are, humbled through our disappointments and personal failings, yet having the audacity to reach out to the divine.

Even as you rear back in pain, you stand on the threshold of the holy. The same impulse that puts words of complaint into your mind is now urging you to turn your complaints into prayer.

The complaints in this entry are a contemporary interpretation of Psalms 69:1–5.

11

Envision the Best Possible Outcome, Too

At the moment of impact, it is natural to focus on your fears. *What's going to happen to me? What else is going to go wrong now? How am I to survive?*

You think you are being realistic, facing your bleak destiny as if it were cast in stone. But if you are to tell the whole truth, you would have to admit that you don't control the future, any more than you controlled the past. If that is so, it is also true that while you can't stop bad things from happening, you can't stop good things from happening, either. Even as you stand in the shadow of your painful disappointment, if you are honest, you will have to admit that it is just as likely that the best possible outcome will transpire as the worst.

Everyone has moments of forgetfulness, when they believe all is lost. More than anything in the world, the young Franklin D. Roosevelt wanted to be a writer. He wrote a story about the life of John Paul Jones and sent it to a movie producer. When it came back rejected, he thought he was finished and would never amount to anything. Thomas Edison failed a thousand times before producing a lightbulb that actually worked.

Just because you fear the worst does not mean you need to let your emotions call the shots in your life. No matter how embedded in concrete your fear seems to be to you right now, understand that everything—including your feelings—is in constant motion. Just as night turns into day, drought to flood, so it is that at the peak of your fear or sorrow, you may suddenly burst into the fresh air of expanded perspective. However you are feeling right now—it will pass. Emotions are like the weather. A storm of upset may be hard upon you. You've got a choice. You can grab a cup of tea and snuggle by the fire, waiting for it to wear itself out; you can rush outside unprotected, grumbling against it as you go; or you can put on your boots and begin to splash around. It is the nature of the universe that, sooner or later, weather more to your liking is bound to arrive.

Our futures are open. Everything is always in motion. Hope takes this into consideration, choosing to believe that regardless of how you are feeling at any given moment, the most optimistic outcomes are still possible. Many influences will contribute to the resolution, and your very hope becomes one of those determining factors. Perhaps it is but a very small consideration, but even so, it may carry just enough weight to make all the difference.

Just because this disappointment has happened in your life doesn't mean that you won't yet end up with a future far greater than what the past indicates is probable for you. Always be prepared for anything—but expect only the best.

12

Exercise Your Spirit

*H*aving extended heartfelt hospitality to the Hasidic master Baal Shem Tov, the oil merchant Rachamim was granted the blessing of his choice. Already living in comfort and peace, he had but one wish: a guaranteed place in the world to come. Hearing this, the Baal Shem Tov sighed deeply, replying at last, "Assemble a large shipment of wine and bring it to my home."

This was no small task, given that the Baal Shem Tov lived far from Rachamim. But the oil merchant complied, leading his caravan of carts and drivers through towns, villages, and forests. One night, as rain suddenly burst from the heavens, Rachamim hurried down the road to find shelter for his load. Settling the carts and drivers into a large, empty warehouse, he then returned to an inn nearby to pass the night. In the morning, he rose early to rejoin his caravan, but something was terribly amiss. The warehouse was empty. There was no sign of the wine, the wagons, or the drivers. He hurried back to the inn, but it, too, had disappeared. Spying a group of men talking by the roadside, he hurried over to them: "Have I lost my way? Where is the inn of this village?"

The men looked at him, amused. "There is no inn near here," they replied.

Rachamim took the news heavily, sinking to the ground. "What am I to do?" he cried. He was far from home and family, having lost everything. As he lay in the dust, a group of beggars happened by and invited him to join them. Rachamim assented, never once succumbing to bitterness about his great loss.

The band of beggars wandered from village to village, arriving after many months at the hometown of the Baal Shem Tov. Sensing Rachamim's arrival, the Baal Shem Tov sent for him, preparing for him at his table the seat of honor.

"Do you remember the last time we met?" the Baal Shem Tov asked him at last. "You asked me for a share in the world to come. You believed that all you needed was my blessing. But my blessing, alone, could not prepare you for that which you've asked."

The Baal Shem Tov explained to those who had gathered that Rachamim had impressed him with his heartfelt hospitality. But having a good heart alone is not enough to warrant a place in the world to come. If one has a pleasant life, goodness can come easily. But to have everything taken away and not become bitter, this is how one becomes worthy of the blessing that Rachamim desired.

The Baal Shem Tov continued, "On Sunday, Rachamim's wagons, wine, and drivers will find their ways back to him."

Sure enough, just as the Baal Shem Tov promised, Rachamim's worldly goods were restored to him. But as happy as he was to have them back, they meant little compared to his greatest attainment: a heart that had shown itself strong enough to sing a song of sweetness and hope regardless of whatever fate sent his way.

This retelling was inspired by Sterna Citron, daughter of the late Rabbi Eli Chaim Carlebach.

Time to Regroup

> "Though not the master of one's fate, one may still be captain of one's soul."
>
> —Philip Brickman

You fear you are alone. But it is the essence of divine love that is manifesting in your heart as the craving for resilience. The emotional pain you feel contains the seed of the answers you are seeking: wisdom beyond that which logic and rational thought could produce, resources you did not know you had. As the initial impact of what has happened to you recedes, you begin to find opportunities to nurture your spirit at the deepest levels. Cultivate within yourself qualities of character, such as strength, faith, and perseverance, and you will fortify yourself for the greater role you are being prepared to play in the world.

13

Change Only What You Must

Why are you hurrying so? Do you think that if you figure everything out, assess every possible ramification, quickly shore up the cracks and throw a new building up on the rubble your misfortune has left behind, you can minimize what has happened? Do you really believe that upon this hastily repaired foundation, you can build a structure so mighty that nothing will ever touch you again?

Soon you will have the opportunity to build anew. But if you want your new construction to better withstand the winds of fate, build slowly this time. Obstacles that obstruct your passion are not always a bad thing. It can be to your advantage to work under such pressure. Let your sorrow deepen your foundation. Sift through your broken dreams to retrieve materials made from the strength of experience. Gather the information you need to make a better plan that builds resilience and flexibility into the design.

How fortunate are you who are courageous enough to give your life the gift of time—the anvil upon which your character, strength, ability, and passion can be forged for purposes beyond what you have imagined for yourself. When the time comes to begin again, you will bring an artist's deft touch to the loving placement of every brick, plank, and nail.

If there is something you must do right away—some action this situation requires of you—of course you must rise to the occasion. Deal with the situations and options that present themselves to you one by one. But do only what you must. Resist the urge to make any more changes than necessary until you are truly ready. Even as your will cries out to you to take decisive action, lay down your hammers and saws and sit quietly, patiently, amid the debris. Watch, listen, and wait. When your time has come to act, nobody will be able to stop you—not lost time nor missed opportunities nor unjust systems. The moment will come. Certain and true. It will come.

14

Take an Emotional Vacation

Circumstances could not have looked any bleaker for the apostle Paul, as recounted in the Book of Acts. Taken as prisoner aboard a ship in the midst of a fierce winter storm, he found the vessel soon caught in a violent wind rushing down from Crete. Pounded by the storm, the prisoners were instructed to begin throwing the cargo overboard. Surrounded by darkness so thick, that neither sun nor stars had broken through in many days, the captain and crew abandoned all hope of being saved. What did Paul do? He urged everyone to break out the bread and have a bite.

At that moment, a return to normalcy was exactly what was called for. Revitalized by their respite, the men were better able to deal with the ramifications of their situation. Soon thereafter, the ship broke up into pieces, but all on board managed to make their way safely to land.

Some years ago, when my husband, Dan, and I were running a public-relations agency together in San Francisco, one of our most trusted employees suddenly gave us notice that she was leaving to set up a competitive firm, taking some of our key people and accounts with her. The pain and fear nearly overwhelmed us. Not only that we wouldn't recover from the loss—but whom could we ever trust again? Our first response was to rush together some help-wanted ads. Talk to the lawyer about lawsuits. Send out new business letters to every company in town. But as fast as we rushed about, shoring up the breaches, the faster the emotional waters of resentment, sadness, and fear poured into the hull. So what did we do? Dan and I cashed in our frequent-flier miles and headed to Hawaii for five days.

For the first three or four days, we basked on the beach, drank piña coladas, and adroitly avoided any discussion related to the incident. We were quite simply not ready to face the pain yet. When we spoke of anything related to our livelihood at all, it was to day-dream about a more perfect future. Somehow, as we resolutely turned away from the wreckage we had left behind, hope was quietly, secretly—unbeknownst to us—being restored. By the end of the five days, we were strong enough to face our situation and begin to respond to the challenges that fate presented to us.

I suppose there were those who whispered about our sad little escape from our troubles. If we had tried to put our thinking into words, we would have responded that what we were doing was, in fact, surrendering control over the situation, in order to allow our spirits to begin to heal at their own pace and in their own way. It took more courage for us to break out the bread and throw an emotional vacation for ourselves than it would have had we chosen to stay put and try to bail ourselves out with our badly broken buckets. For five glorious days, we trusted that our destiny would continue to move us toward recovery, with or without our conscious participation.

It didn't hurt that we had the means and opportunity to take our emotional vacation in Hawaii. But there are many ways you can break out the bread, even as the ship beneath you is going to pieces. You can throw yourself into aspects of your work or life that have not been touched by your disappointment. You can treat yourself to a weekend with the phone off the hook and a refrigerator full of Chinese takeout. You can close the windows of your car as you drive to work, singing as loud as you can to classic rock and roll. It doesn't matter what other people think of you. If you need to take an emotional vacation, you need only act as if everything is going to turn out somehow in the end. You know why? Because somehow or other, it will.

15

Let Your Yearning Grow Larger Than Your Fear

*R*ight now, you may be feeling estranged and alone in an uncaring universe. You may fear that you have been abandoned, that pieces of you have been dealt away in failure or shame. In the depths of your dark night, you yearn for wholeness.

In your present mood, it is easy to question whether fortune has turned away from you, leaving you to stumble alone through the abyss. Perhaps you fear that this is so, that resolution is always to be beyond your grasp. It is the same feeling as when you are homesick. Separated from home and from those who love you, yearning settles heavily upon your heart. Part of you has been left behind as you ache for reconciliation. But consider this: When you are homesick, you can feel pain only because you know what home means, and what it is to be loved.

Just as homesickness points to your experience of a real home, real love, so does your yearning contain the memory of what has also already truly been yours. It is your unrest, itself, that proclaims the truth that wholeness of spirit is real and possible. You can feel this way only because you know what connection to the divine means, and what it is to be loved by God.

You fear you are alone. But in truth, it is the essence of divine love, itself, manifesting in your heart as the craving for something more, guiding you forward to gather into your spirit that which is already yours. The greatness of your yearning gives testimony to the depth of your connection to the divine.

In truth, it is as the mystics teach: You would not seek if you had not already been found.

16

Ask Your Pain for Answers

When your body hurts, the physician inventories your symptoms in order to determine the best course of action to take.

The emotional pain you feel when you are faced with a disappointment also contains important information. What is the nature and severity of the upset? How well are you equipped to respond to it? What do you need to heal? If you are willing to engage actively with your pain, you will avail yourself of emotional wisdom beyond that which logic and rational thinking could produce.

You can begin here, now, by answering these questions. To enhance the effectiveness of this process, I suggest that you write down your responses. Write as quickly as possible, not worrying about logic or grammar. Let your words ride your emotion onto the page. If you feel stuck for an answer, or if you find yourself thinking things through analytically rather than emotionally, switch your pen to your recessive hand and continue writing. Spend a few minutes on each question.

What is the nature of your disappointment?

1. Can you identify a specific incident or occasion that precipitated your pain, or is the cause of a diffuse or general nature?
2. Is your pain related to life-cycle events or to untimely and unexpected occurrences you could not have anticipated?
3. Is your concern for yourself or does your pain derive from your concern for others?
4. Do you believe it came about, at least in part, as the result of some shortcoming on your part?
5. As a result of your disappointment, has your idea about yourself, how the world works, about others, or about your relationship to the divine been impacted? What did you used to believe? What do you believe now?

What is the severity of the situation?

6. Does the disappointment impact your means of survival? Your role or identity?
7. What are your biggest concerns about the situation?
8. Can you trust yourself at this time to make a realistic assessment of the severity of your situation, or has your perspective been distorted by unsupported fears about the future? Are you oversimplifying? Overgeneralizing?

9. Is any anger or fear you are feeling being expressed to a degree appropriate to the objective threat or impact?

10. What hasn't been impacted by this situation?

How well are you equipped to respond to the situation?

11. How have you resolved similar situations in the past? What can you apply to your current situation? What is different about this time?

12. Do you feel that you have the emotional, spiritual, mental, and physical resources necessary to bring about the resolution you seek? Do you have sufficient information? If not, what area(s) is lacking?

13. If there is a discrepancy between what is needed and your ability or willingness to respond, are you able to accept this situation, or must you seek outside help?

What will it take for you to heal?

14. Rather than asking you to respond to specific questions related to this topic, set aside ten minutes to respond in writing using the techniques described above. Don't judge your responses. Write everything that comes into your mind. If you feel stuck, write down, "I feel stuck." Don't be afraid of anything that emerges from your pen. Follow your emotions wherever they may lead. Pain, grieving, and anger are not an illness or a problem, but rather, a way of working through the ramifications of your disappointments.

17

There Is Always Something You Can Do

The *I Ching* explains that life is sometimes like a well that is being lined with stone. While it is true that the well cannot be used while the work is going on, "the work is not in vain; the result is that the water stays clear. In life also there are times when a man must put himself in order."

There are times when you feel invisible. You feel passed over and ineffective. Your phone messages go unanswered. Your letters come back to you marked address unknown. During such times, you may not be able to express your power in the outer world. But that does not mean that you have the right to throw up your hands in despair.

Rather, you can take this opportunity to enhance your character through the serious work of inner development. What you are doing may not be apparent on the surface. It may look as if you have fallen into disuse. But the work that is transpiring in you at this very moment, so quiet and so internal that even you may not have realized it was going on, is of utmost importance. What you are doing when you give yourself the time and space to nurture your spirit at the deepest levels is no less than fortifying yourself for the greater role you are being prepared to play in the world. The *I Ching* teaches that if you cultivate within yourself qualities of character, such as strength, faith, and perseverance, you will not have to force opportunities to come to you. Those that are meant to be yours will come to you of their own free will.

"When the quiet power of a man's own character is at work, the effects produced are right. All those who are receptive to the vibrations of such a spirit will then be influenced."

There will be a time when people will come again to your well, and the water you will have for them will be clear and sweet.

18

Listen for the Lyrics

*E*very disappointment has a song. As you drive to work or do the dishes, listen for the music that is humming in your mind. The lyrics of your special song will help you grasp the true nature of your pain and indicate to you how best to proceed.

How can this be?

Each of us contains both right-brain and left-brain capabilities. Your left brain encompasses your logical, rational ability to assess a situation, weigh the pros and cons, and make choices. Scientists postulate that the left hemisphere of your brain is responsible for logic, language, and linear thought. We tend to depend on our left-brain processes, particularly when we are faced with a problem, because we want to get back in control. In our action-oriented society, we are most comfortable with our left-brain capability's urge for order. But understand this. The left brain's powers are limited to building upon the thoughts, ideas, and information that are already present in your consciousness. Your left brain can only add on to existing structures.

At the same time that your left brain is busily processing your upset, your right brain has been faithfully gathering new evidence, data, experience, and ideas that can provide the key to the healing you've been searching for. Your intuitive right brain is the creator of your breakthroughs, sudden clarity, realizations, and insights.

But your right brain works quietly. It does not press you forward into action. It waits patiently for you, just beneath the surface of your conscious mind. It is the fragment of the dream that lingers in the morning. The unrecognized inspiration that expresses itself as vague yearning. The forgotten name that pops into your mind when you least expect it. The music in your soul. The right hemisphere of your brain is, even as you read this paragraph, generating intuition, knowledge, and guidance beyond that which your logic can access. It is operating in you right now, just waiting for you to tune in.

In order to tap this wellspring of wisdom, you need only release the grip of your logical thought processes for a moment. Like a camera shifting its focus, new information will suddenly reveal itself to you.

What is your right brain trying to get through to you? You'll know it when you can hear its song. The song you catch yourself humming bears a message for you to decipher. Your intuitive right brain is singing its wisdom to you now. Can you hear it?

19

Rerun the Upset, Imagining Everyone Involved to Be Four Years Old

Many years ago, our public-relations company was hired by the marketing director of one of San Francisco's largest office and retail complexes. At the time, I believed we had been chosen for this plum appointment because we were the best and brightest agency around. In retrospect, I have come to believe we landed the job primarily because, being young, we could be counted on to do twice the work of anyone else in town—for half the price.

Not knowing this at the time, I ended up at an important social function attended not only by the marketing director, but by the president of the company himself. Having heard that the president had recently been named to a prestigious board, I heartily extended my hand to him in congratulation. He turned briskly away, leaving my hand dangling in midair. Later, the marketing director angrily informed me that I had offended the president by addressing him by his first name. I spent most of the party feeling deeply embarrassed.

But toward the end of this sad little affair, I caught a glimpse of the president across the room. He was surrounded by his peers—middle-aged men with protruding bellies poorly disguised beneath look-alike gray pin-striped suits. All of a sudden, I felt myself back on a nursery-school playground looking at the class bully, a chubby-cheeked fellow of no more than, say, four years of age, surrounded by his diapered minions. I could barely suppress the giggle that threatened to emerge. For even as I saw the president revealed fully to me at his true emotional age, I recognized his cronies as if they, too, were no more than four years old. The marketing director fell next to my vision, afraid that the teacher was going to tell her parents that she had done something wrong. Then, like dominoes on a rug, the entire social constellation of partygoers suddenly transformed into a room full of preschoolers.

Empowered by this vision, I felt my strength quickly pour back into me. My disappointment was being played out in a room full of toddlers. We may have been in dress-up clothes, doing grown-up-looking things, but emotionally, I was dealing with the same kinds of issues that I'd been dealing with since nursery school. The class kiss-up, the tattletale, the bully, the wimp.

But then, who was I? Where did I fit into the picture? Was I the same four-year-old who longed to run home crying to Mother because the bad president refused to shake my hand? Had anything at all changed—if not for the bullies in the room, at least for me?

Suddenly, I recognized within myself the four-year-old, not as a shameful failure, but rather, as the courageous risk taker who so often tried so hard to get things right—and who sometimes fell short of her expectations. In many ways, I was that same courageous little girl. But there was something new. For as I looked at the four-year-old in myself, shivering in shame, I found myself spontaneously embracing her with compassion. It was all going to be all right. I would grow up and start a business that would have good moments and bad. I would do uninformed things sometimes, and I would correct my mistakes and move on. I would learn to separate the true from the false. And someday, I would even stumble into a room full of business associates who were emotionally frozen at the nursery-school level, and I would end up feeling empathy for myself and possibly even the hints of a glimmer for them.

When I left the party, I successfully fought down the urge to spin a spitball in the president's direction. I went on to complete the project with the style and dignity worthy of someone who could build on life's lessons, while remembering vividly the vulnerability of how it feels to be a child.

20

Clean Up Your Address Book

The last thing you may feel like doing is reaching out to somebody for comfort or help. You are so vulnerable right now. It is no coincidence that the root word for *vulnerable* is the Latin word for *wound*. Just as an injured bear retreats to its cave to lick its wounds, so may you intuit that you need the time and space at this moment to heal privately. There is natural wisdom if your heart is urging you to take yourself out of circulation for a while.

Not only when faced with distressing circumstances, but periodically throughout their adult years, the African Kikuyu go off to the bush alone for extended periods in order to "let their souls catch up with their bodies." Isolating to heal is a short-term response to disappointment that bears with it the body wisdom of natural healing.

But it is also possible that your urge to isolate yourself derives more from fear that you will not be understood, that your deepest wounds will go untended or, worse, rejected, should you bare your sorrows. And yet, you have been there for others. Over time, you have tended the needs of many of your friends and family. Chances are that you have forgotten how many people you have touched in your life over the years. There were those times you lent a warm shoulder for someone to cry on. You listened to someone as long as he or she needed to talk. You went out of your way to help somebody.

And at the same time, others have been there for you as well. Who have you forgotten that may have advice or resources that could be useful to you? Somebody who might know a good financial planner or therapist? Who has gone through a disappointment similar to your own who will understand how you feel? Is there somebody you can trust to let yourself fall apart around?

Your address book is filled with possibilities—acquaintances who have not yet been tapped but who you intuit are capable of meaningful exchange. Chances are that your files contain many forgotten and untapped resources. While you may well decide to honor your urge to be alone right now, there will be a time, perhaps sooner than you anticipate, when you will want to turn to others you trust for emotional support. You may want someone to confide in. Someone to socialize with who will help you take your mind off your problems for a while. Somebody to guide you or to give you practical assistance.

Take this opportunity to update your contacts. After you have purged your system of individuals who are no longer a desired part of your support network, go through the names again. This time, take note of anybody whom you feel warmly about. If you feel so moved, go ahead and give them a call. You can tell them all about what happened to you—or you can simply call to get an update on their fax number, and see what happens.

21

Take a Notebook to a Cafe and Write the Story of Your Life

You have been in tight spots before—and yet somehow you made it through. At the time, you thought it was all over for you, and yet you somehow found it in your heart to keep on going. There have been moments of supreme joy—and moments of deep despair. Sometimes you thought it was all over for you—that there was no hope for the future. And yet, something always came along to get you going again.

And you learned from your disappointments. Not just once, but over and over again. You can now see that individuals or situations in your life that caused you great pain also taught you important things about yourself and the way of the world. Youthful innocence deepened with time, as your experience of life became richer for your having gone through the many challenges you have faced.

There was the destiny of your birth, which placed you with a certain family and in particular circumstances. There were the tragedies that dulled the edges of your arrogance, giving you depth and compassion. There were brave choices made, and there were poor decisions. Things happened to you that you could not possibly have anticipated. Certainly there were mistakes you made that you never need make again. Others have made mistakes, as well.

But you have had wonderful things happen to you, too: twists and turns of fate that sent you off on adventures you could not have anticipated. In fact, if you were to put the events of your life in the hands of a great writer, you would soon see yourself as the hero of your own life story, a life filled with challenges and possibilities. And why not? Why not extend to yourself the dignity of placing your current situation into the greater perspective of the grand sweep of generations? There is a great writer in you ready to tell the tale. In the tradition of F. Scott Fitzgerald. Dostoyevsky. Danielle Steele. Dress yourself in a black turtleneck and jeans, swing a scarf over your shoulders, head for the corner table of a cafe that serves steaming cafe lattes, and write the story of your life.

Here's how to start. Identify ten turning points in your life. You were born, you went to a certain school, you met somebody who would play an important role in your life. . . . What are the ten most important events of your life to date? After you've identified ten pivotal events, make each the title of a chapter in your autobiography. "Chapter One: The Little Princess Makes Her Grand

Entrance" or "Whoops! Where Did He Come From?" Whatever it is that expresses the mood of that time in your life.

Now fill out the chapters as completely and imaginatively as possible, not worrying so much about factual details as about capturing your experiences. To get you going, here are some questions you might find helpful to address:

What is a particular memory I have from that time of my life that captures the flavor of my experience?

Could I have done anything more or different about the situation, given the circumstances I faced, where I came from, and what I knew then?

What did this situation teach me about myself, about others, about life?

What happened as a result of this situation that I could not have anticipated?

How is it that the thing that happened so long ago relates to the pain I am facing today?

What do I know now that I didn't know then?

After you've completed these ten chapters, turn to the next blank page and write in big, bold print, "The Story of My Life: Part Two." Remember that your masterpiece, no matter how many pages you have written, is but a work in progress. You cannot yet know what all of the things that have happened to you in your life signify, what they are leading to. As much as you have already lived, there is more to go. And how rich and exciting the future will be! For as you read between the lines of your life to date, surely you can appreciate the courage, the depth of feeling, the willingness to pick up the pieces and try again, evidenced on page after page. Given how much you had going for you in the past, with all this new experience and knowledge under your belt, think how much more equipped you will now be to handle life's twists and turns. Your greatest achievements, your greatest joys, your greatest contributions lie ahead of you. The blank pages beckon you to build on your experiences of the past, totally receptive to new adventures beyond anything you have yet envisioned for yourself. Just as disappointments in the past led you into new directions beyond your judgment and expectation, so does this challenge bring you to the threshold of a whole new world of possibilities.

Your story is unfinished. You are still in the middle of writing the book. It is way too soon to judge how things turned out for you.

Signs of Spring

"The important thing is not to think much, but to love much; and so do that which best stirs you to love."

—SAINT TERESA OF AVILA

Everything is in a constant state of change. At this moment, you may feel that winter has bared your branches. But neither you nor anyone else can judge what is really going on with you by looking only at your external manifestations. How reluctantly you shed the vivid colors of autumn, now enriching the soil of your roots. Beneath your naked limbs, new life is being readied to blossom forth. When you are fully alive, you are continually asked to let go of what you have in order to prepare the way for new possibilities to come to you. Tend what is passing, but put your energy into what is birthing. As you do, you put forces in motion that will bring to you new strength, courage, and opportunities.

22

Model Your Life on the Spiral, Not the Stick

"As long as man's inner nature remains inwardly
stronger and richer than anything fate brings
his way, good fortune will not desert him.
For the superior man everything furthers—
even descent."

—THE *I CHING*

In the Western model of success, we are taught that progress is a vertical climb from obscurity to prominence. The ascent should be flawless. Every life event should represent a brisk stride forward. All you need to do is to work hard, be smart, and keep your eyes focused on what you want. If you have to push through your fears and feelings, you do so. If you have to set aside your values or ignore the urge to nurture yourself or others, so be it.

There is a problem with this model, the model of the stick, for when you commit yourself to letting nothing get in your way, you become brittle and reactive. You set yourself against the universe, inadvertently increasing resistance to your efforts by the nature of your rigid stance.

Wouldn't it be better if there were a model of success that didn't view pain as an aberration—but rather, as a healthy part of a successful life process? Happily, we have access to the wisdom of Eastern philosophy to provide us with the alternative we seek. More than three thousand years ago, the ancient seers of China developed a philosophy of success based not on the model of the line, but of the spiral. Capturing their wisdom in the *I Ching*, the ancient Chinese developed their concept by observing the cycles of nature.

They noticed that everything in nature is in a constant state of change. Just when a season or stage reaches its peak, it inevitably turns into its opposite. Fall dies to winter, preparing the soil for the rebirth of spring, culminating in summer. Summer fades into the fall, starting the cycle over and over again. Living creatures are born, mature, give birth, and then die. From the rich soil of their graves sprout seeds of new life. You cannot judge the truth of the seasons by staying only on the surface. You must live many years, gain the perspective of many seasons, to be able to comprehend the real work that is taking place at any given time.

So it is in your life. Right now, you may feel that winter has bared your branches. But neither you nor anyone else can judge what is really going on with you by looking only at your external manifestations. Sometimes, you are on the upswing, feeling the warmth of the sunlight opening your leaves. Sometimes, you will be turned away, to navigate the downward slope of the spiral.

These are the days you experience as decay and dissolution. But even these dark days are necessary for the spiral to continue its ascent. In nature, destruction often is the requisite state that precedes new growth, like the bursting open of a pinecone in the heat of a forest fire, releasing its seeds to the soil. When you are fully alive, you are continually asked to let go of what you have in order to make space for new possibilities to come to you. But notice, this model is not a circle, the repetition of endless births and deaths, going nowhere, accomplishing nothing. No, this is an expanding spiral, each turn of the spiral grown stronger, larger, fed by the enriched soil of your experiences, your learnings, and yes, even your setbacks. You free your essential spirit from the need to protect what you had, and relax into an expanded vision of your true human potential. There is growth, there is progress. But it is advancement not despite your challenges, but including them.

Rather than saying that you will succeed, allowing nothing to get in your way, mastering the art of resilience requires you to do whatever it takes, understanding that many things are going to get in your way.

23

Give Yourself Roses in Winter

Just as the cycles of nature are inevitable, so is it inevitable that you will have cycles of birthing and dying in your own life. You cannot stop the waning and waxing of your life spiral. But there is something you can do. You can stay alert, even in the depths of winter, for signs of spring. When they appear to you, invest them with your vital energy. You need not ignore that which is dying. You tend that which is passing from you and your life responsibly and dutifully. But put your energy into what is birthing.

Regardless of where you are on the spiral's bend, you can surround yourself with symbols of new life. Put a vase full of pussy willows on your desk. Indulge yourself with pots of blossoms on your windowsills. Send yourself flowers. Water all of the plants in your house. Spend the day working in your garden.

As you watch for signs of new life, let yourself be curious. What will take root in this rich, warm mud?

Tend what is passing and put your attention on that which presses to be born.

24

Do Something
You Loved as a Child

Legend has it that before the discovery of antibiotics, Ivan Pavlov, the great proponent of behavioral psychology, was overtaken by a life-threatening infection. As he lay dying in his bed, consumed by the raging fever, he managed to deliver a seemingly delusional request to his assistant. He asked his aide to go down to the river near his home, and return with a big bucket of sun-warmed mud. Humoring Pavlov, the aide duly brought the bucket of mud to his bed. Shaky and weak, the great behaviorist dipped his hands into the bucket and started to play with the oozy brown clay. Within a few hours, Pavlov's fever finally broke.

Hearing the story years later, many have wondered if Pavlov had intuited the presence of some natural antibiotic properties in river mud. But his explanation for his odd behavior was of a some-what different nature. Pavlov explained that as a child, he had often gone down to the riverbank with his mother. While she did the laundry, he enjoyed playing near her with the clay of the riverbank. As he played in the mud, she would tell him wonderful stories. This memory represented for him the time in his life when he felt most peaceful. As he lay ill in bed, he reasoned that if he could re-create this favorite time in his life, he would give his body the best chance to recover.

You, too, are longing for the fever of your pain to break. There comes a time when you must take the recovery of your emotions into your own hands. You can begin this process by asking yourself what it was that you loved to do as a child. Did you used to build forts out of sticks in your backyard? Finger-paint pictures of mon-sters and angels? Dance to rock and roll on your dining-room table? To help you jog your memory, you might want to go to your old scrapbooks and look at pictures of yourself as a child. Did you love building snowmen? Snuggling with the family dog? If you've played with the notion of buying in-line skates or bringing home a new puppy from the pound, this could well be the time for you to take the plunge. Whatever it is that you remember most fondly, do it now. As you consider the possibility of re-creating your favorite memory here and now, you may find yourself worrying that in the face of the gravity of your situation, you are simply being self-indulgent or silly. But in truth, by fulfilling your childish whim, you may well be embarking upon the fastest and most effective route to recovery.

25

Solve Something

In the wake of your misfortune, chances are that you have over-drawn your internal self-esteem savings account. Here's how it works. When something good happens to you, it is like putting money in the bank. Achieve a goal, keep a commitment, rectify a wrong, and you are putting credits into the bank. When you have substantial savings built up, you have self-esteem reserves to draw upon when times are lean. But if the extremity of the situation you are facing has caused you to withdraw more than your account contained, you will find yourself unhappily in the red. The way back to emotional health is to begin making investments back into your self-esteem account.

Recently, I had a call from a colleague of mine named Joan.

Her husband of fifteen years had just left her for a younger woman. For many years, despite many valiant attempts, Joan had been unable to become pregnant. In fact, part of her husband's explanation for his betrayal was his desire to find someone who could give him a son. Joan's esteem had been devastated. Unable to work, she turned in her resignation and had taken to wandering listlessly around her house. Following her best friends' advice, she decided to ask her doctor to put her on an antidepressant drug like Prozac. While she was sitting in her doctor's waiting room, she opened up an old magazine with a crossword puzzle on the back page. Miraculously, the puzzle had not been filled in. Passing the time, Joan dug into her purse, pulled out her pen, and set to work. Turned out, she was pretty good at it. By the time the nurse called her name, she had completed the puzzle. Despite herself, when she was face-to-face with her physician, she had a hard time suppressing her feelings of satisfaction over this little accomplishment. The thought dawned in her that the crossword puzzle was a sign that perhaps her innate ability to recover would soon be kicking in. Together, she and her physician agreed that she should put off the Prozac for a while.

On the way home, she stopped by the bookstore and bought herself a whole book of crossword puzzles. For weeks, she did little else but sit by the fire in her living room, working the puzzles. When she finished the first book, she quickly returned for another, more challenging one.

Her call came into me soon after she had cracked what was considered to be the most difficult book of crossword puzzles on the market. She felt, at last, ready to reenter the mainstream of her life. In fact, she had called me looking for job leads. As she caught me up to date, she explained that through the simple act of completing her crosswords, she had gotten herself back into the black. She was ready to begin filling in the blanks of her own life, and solving crossword puzzles had shown her the way.

If you are feeling depleted, set yourself an achievable goal. You can start small. In fact, the secret to recovery is simple: You can start anywhere. The important thing is to make your beginning. If you don't know where to begin, start the only place you can: where you are. Look around the room where you are right now. Could the books on the shelf use straightening? How about taking that walk you've been promising yourself? Buy an electronic chess set and progress through the levels, or think of a favor you could do for a friend. Find something you know you can solve—and solve it now.

When you begin, you put forces in motion that will bring to you new strength, courage, and opportunities.

26

Treat Yourself as You Would a Best Friend

*I*f this disappointment had happened to somebody you loved, would you be saying the kinds of things to him or her that you are saying to yourself? Would you be harsh and strident, or would you be warm and comforting? Would you be impatient with his or her grieving, or would you be compassionate and understanding?

Now is the time to be kind to yourself. There's no need to get to the bottom of things before you take this assignment on. And you don't have to wait until tomorrow, hoping to find the right side of your bed. Treat yourself as if you were your own best friend and resilience is but one act of generosity away. Buy something silly from a street artist and give it to yourself. Send yourself little love notes. Hide them in drawers where you will stumble across them days later when you could use a reminder of how cherished you are. Take yourself out for the day, going to your favorite lunch spot and letting yourself pick the movie you most want to see. Feed even the dimmest inkling of healing with lavish praise and support. You deserve to have as good a friend as you.

27

Find Something for Which You Can Feel Grateful

Once upon a time, there was an elderly couple who had raised one child, a daughter. She had been everything to them, and they doted upon her. The girl had gold, curly hair and she ran about the yard chasing grasshoppers in the sunlight. In the evening, she danced for them by the warm glow of the fire.

Every year, on the anniversary of the day of the child's birth, the old man went out to the fields to gather colorful bouquets of her favorite flowers. When he returned, he scrubbed every corner of their little cottage, placing the flowers everywhere. The old woman cooked the child her favorite supper and baked her a great birthday cake.

All was well until the girl turned sixteen. So lovely and happy was she that she caught the eye of a prince from a faraway land, passing through their village on his way home from war. He asked her to be his bride, promising her wealth and riches beyond anything she had ever imagined. But there was a catch: She would never see her parents again.

While her parents could never deny to her what would bring her happiness, they could not bear the thought of life without her. They spoke to her of the village boys, any of whom would have been glad to marry her. They sang to her the songs of her childhood and gathered the flowers and foods that they knew she loved. But the girl had made up her mind to go. Even though she loved her parents, her destiny beckoned her into the unknown. She and her parents clung to one another weeping, but the prince soon lifted her onto his stallion and they rode off and away. The parents never saw their daughter again.

Year after year, as the sun set on the fields, the old man and the old woman would walk out to the dusty road and sigh longingly after the girl. On her birthday, they would put on black clothes and sit in the dark. Their hearts broken, they thought only of their great loss.

Then the old man took ill. The village doctor looked in upon him, offering herbal brews and potions. But nothing seemed to help. The days dragged on, one after the other. Soon it would be the anniversary of their daughter's birth. The old woman knew that in his weakened state, the old man could not survive the day's intense grieving over the memory of their loss. But suddenly, the old woman had an idea.

As the day approached, she became very busy. She dusted and

mended the cottage, which had fallen into disrepair. She went out into the fields and gathered bouquets of flowers. Then she returned to the kitchen and began to bake. "Old woman. What are you doing?" the man whispered from his straw bed.

"For all these years, we have grieved the memory of our loss," she replied. "But not this year. This year, we are going to celebrate the memory of the great joy we have had."

With that, she served her husband a great big piece of the most beautiful birthday cake that had ever graced a village table. It was exactly the medicine he needed. From that moment on, for the rest of their long, full lives, every year, on the anniversary of their daughter's birth, the old man went up to the fields to gather the prettiest flowers he could find and the old woman baked the best cake she could, and the two celebrated with quiet joy their daughter's birthday together.

28

Tell Your Story to Someone Who Will Listen Quietly

When we are troubled, we often encounter people who have lots of good ideas for us. They seem to know what is on our minds even before we know ourselves. Anything we've been through, they've already experienced and mastered. And as much as you may enjoy having these friends in your life under normal circumstances, when your pain is fresh, do everything in your power to avoid getting trapped in conversation with them. There may come a time when you will want to take advantage of other people's good ideas for you, but in the beginning, look for someone who will simply let you tell your story. What you really need now is someone who will encourage you to give full expression to your feelings and gift you with all the time you need to get through the more difficult material, even if you stumble or hesitate, sit there wordlessly for an uncomfortably long period of time, or retell the same passage over and over again. All you need is one person whose quiet presence reminds you that you have it within yourself to find the answers you need.

Once upon a time in ancient Japan, a young seeker set out to solve the problem of unhappiness. He traveled to many great teachers and heard many wise thoughts, but still he struggled with pain and sorrow. Exhausted at last, he rested for a moment in the garden of the temple. As he sat, a maple leaf broke free from a tree nearby and floated gently to the ground before him. As it fell, the seeker finally had the answer. He bowed before the leaf that had showed him how effortlessly it shared both its front and its backside as it fell, hiding nothing. No self-consciousness, no fear, no shame or regret.

So may you, in the quiet presence of an accepting ear, see your own perceived failures and the universe that let you down as merely the backside of your efforts to be an integral part of the whole of life.

It would be gift enough to find someone to whom you could tell your story and who will simply listen. It would be an added bonus if there's a hug, a hankie, and a big pot of tea involved. Treasure this kind of friend, a listening friend.

29

If You Picked the Wrong
Person to Talk To . . .

*T*ry someone else.

30

Break a Sweat

Choose something you like to do that's good for you, and keep doing it until you exhaust yourself. Dance to your favorite music in the living room. Walk the most challenging path in the park. Wallpaper the bathroom. Something big enough to cause you to break a sweat. If you haven't been doing anything physical for some time, make sure you pick something that will stretch you without injuring yourself.

As you work out, repeat to yourself over and over, "This is one good thing I am doing for myself."

As you get ready for bed, you will feel the vital difference between emotional and physical exhaustion. Tonight, you can get a good night's sleep.

31

Put Yourself Back in the Center of Your Life

Sit quietly until one real, true thing emerges for you to do and then go and do it.

If there are things you need to get rid of, let them go.

If there is something you want for yourself, go get it.

If there's something you know you must do, go do it.

If you need to enlist the support of others, let your needs be known.

If they won't help you, go get it from someone who will.

If you are tired of being good, try being naughty.

When your life is filled up with yourself, then you will be able to give to others out of your fullness rather than your neediness. There will be no stopping you—all the good you can do.

32

Create Your Own
Calendar of Holidays

Can you think of anybody who has suffered a misfortune similar to yours, and handled themself and the situation in an admirable way? If so, dedicate a day in your calendar to celebrate that individual. You could pick somebody who probably doesn't think of him- or herself in heroic terms. Morris Fisher, for example, who was a friend of your sister's who got fired from his job as an accountant after twenty years and without batting an eye went back to school to change careers and is now the town's hottest hairdresser. March 21: Happy Morris Fisher Day!

If you've found yourself at odds with prevailing opinions a lot lately, for example, wouldn't it be helpful to honor the birthday of somebody who was willing to put his very life on the line for the sake of the truth? February 19 is Nicolaus Copernicus's birth anniversary.

Ever had to deal with ridicule? How about celebrating December 1, Julia A. Davis Moore's birth anniversary. Who's Julia Moore? "Chase's Annual Events" reports that back at the turn of the century, Moore was a popular author and orator of tragic ballads. During one of her many public recitations, the audience was so moved by her performance, they sprang to their feet, breaking out in wild ovation. A newspaper account reports: "Pandemonium broke loose in the galleries. The crowd shouted and stamped its feet." What was it about this tragic ballad that moved them so? The newspaper report continues: Her poems were "so bad, her subjects so morbid and her naivete so genuine" they were appreciated as contributions of unintentional but wildly hysterical genius. Upon the occasion of her retirement, she informed her audience glibly, "You people paid fifty cents to see a fool, but I got fifty dollars to look at a house full of fools."

However it is you arrive at your special days, add them into your calendar and celebrate them as your own personal holidays.

33

Set Miracles in Motion

*I*n a moment of trial, Daniel asked God to respond to his fervent prayers for help. And for twenty-one days, Daniel waited for his prayers to be answered. Humbly, with all the goodness of his heart, he kept the hope alive that God would send him the guidance he needed. As day after day passed, his strength left him. His complexion grew deathly pale.

And then, after twenty-one days, an angel came to him. The angel appeared before Daniel and so it was that Daniel stood before the angel trembling. The angel spoke to him.

"Do not fear, Daniel, for from the first day that you set your mind to gain understanding and to humble yourself before your God, your words have been heard, and I have come because of your words."

From the very first day, the angel had intended to deliver his response. But it had taken twenty-one days for this moment to transpire. How could this be?

A fierce battle had broken forth in heaven, the angel explained. Powers and principalities were engaging in combat even as they spoke. That is why he could not respond to Daniel's entreaties for help sooner. The angel reached out to Daniel, saying, "Do not fear, greatly beloved, you are safe. Be strong and courageous!"

Then the angel explained that he must depart quickly, for the battle above was raging unabated and required his speedy return.

From the very first, Daniel had been heard. His cries for help were not in vain.

And so it is that from the very first impulse for good in your heart, you, too, are heard. Even as you read this, your reply is on its way to you.

The good that you do will be answered. If you are afraid you have been overlooked, that all has been for nothing, trust that mysterious forces are nevertheless at work in your life, moving you forward. Your goodness is like the ripples from a skipped rock, setting waves to lap upon the shore of the future.

If you have erred, the purity of your shame, your effort to do better, nevertheless reverberate throughout the universe. Regardless of what has transpired in your life, do not judge that your righteous appeals have gone unfulfilled. Let not impatience dim your fervor. Your heartfelt purity sets forces for good in motion that will make a difference.

34

Let the Embers Catch Fire

Through the ups and downs of the cycles of your life
  and the seasons of the year,
Remember to poke aside the charred wood, trusting that no
  matter how advanced the destruction, there will always
  be one ember yet aglow.

When you find it, tend it with love and hope.
Feed it with your breath,
Dress it with the tender twigs of fresh fuel.
There is always an ember.
Sooner or later, it will catch fire.

The Authentic Life

*"Human beings figure out somewhat more of their
true direction, not by the high stars, but by
stubbing their toes on things stuck in the
mud they are slogging through."*

—CAROLYN GRATTON

True humility is the act of stripping away false notions about yourself and the situations you face in order to deal with what is real. When you have suffered a loss, it takes great strength to tell the whole truth about yourself and the situation, resisting the urge to select only that evidence that validates the least optimistic interpretation of circumstances. Now is the time to be simple. Don't let yourself get swept up in other people's agendas for you, or your own ideas of what your life ought to look like.

35

Keep Things Simple

*I*n ancient India, two disciples debated the comparative merits of their respective gurus.

"My guru is so wonderful. He can do all kinds of miracles," said the first. "He sets up an easel on one side of the river, and paints a picture while standing on the other side. When he meditates, he floats above the ground. When he closes his palm, he materializes precious gems out of thin air. What miracles can your teacher perform?"

The second disciple replied.

"When my master is tired, he sleeps. When he is hungry, he eats."

What kind of miracles are these? To sleep when you are tired?

To eat when you are hungry? The meaning is this. When you have endured a disappointment, it takes great strength of character to be simple. The second disciple's guru teaches us that if you feel bad, feel bad. This is not the same as covering up the truth of your feelings with the empty pretense that you are fine. But neither is it complicating your situation by feeling bad about feeling bad.

It takes great courage to be simple. Are you brave enough to face the true nature and magnitude of what you have suffered? Or could it be that you prefer to exaggerate the seriousness of your situation, selecting evidence that validates only the least optimistic interpretation of circumstances? On the other hand, have you taken refuge in denial, telling yourself that you have accepted the situation, when in truth the time has come to take things seriously?

To be simple requires great self-discipline. Not the cracking of the taskmaster's whip turned harshly against yourself. But rather, the dedication of one's self to becoming a disciple of the truth. True humility is the act of stripping away false notions about yourself and the situation you face in order to deal with what is real.

36

Read Unauthorized Biographies

*E*verybody suffers disappointments. If you are upset that you have not yet found your Prince Charming, anything about Charles and Diana is bound to put your own disappointment in perspective.

All of your problems would be handled, if only you could get your hands on a winning lottery ticket? How about checking out something unauthorized about somebody rich like Donald Trump or Leona Helmsley? As much as the celebrity publicity machine would like you to believe that some of us live more perfect lives than others, it quite simply isn't true.

Everybody has problems. Steven Jobs showed up to be guest lecturer at a college classroom, having just had a fight with his girl-friend. Jack Nicholson's stomach, caught unawares, hangs over his bathing suit. President Bush, at what was supposed to be a high point of his term of office, fell ill at a state dinner and threw up on the lap of the Emperor of Japan.

Okay, so I'm not proud of myself for getting a little thrill at other people's expense. After all, even celebrities deserve our compassion. But first, before we judge ourselves too harshly for indulging ourselves at the expense of others, consider the possibility that there may be a more righteous explanation. After all, we are barraged day after day with images of famous people cooing with their spouses and children in exotic locations, winning awards, looking beautiful. Then we turn back to our own less-than-perfect lives and wonder where we went wrong. If only we could get our hands on their secret. And we can. Because sooner or later, they will pop up on an infomercial somewhere or other, endorsing this or that product that holds the promise of giving us the same protection from the human condition to which they seemingly have been privvy. Her hair spray, his exercise regime. You put in overtime to buy the merchandise that will make you a contender for a rent-free life. Meanwhile, as their perfect white teeth and moist red lips deliver the magic 800 number to call to place your order, your credit-card debit enhances their bottom line.

Wait a day or a year, and the celebrated couple who sold you the tape on relationships with which to enhance your own marriage are on the cover of *People* magazine. Turns out he's a drug addict. She's been beaten. The divorce is final. The hair spray has the same 800 number, but this time, it's some new celebrity offering you a shortcut to happiness.

So go ahead and check out an unauthorized biography—indulge yourself in a wicked day surrounded by all the tabloids on the supermarket shelf—and let yourself gloat. This is not an act of pettiness, but of prophetic indignation, bought and paid for by all the hair spray that turned out to be too stiff to comb.

37

Are You Willing to Pay the Rent?

*E*very fantasy exacts a price.

For years, I had the fantasy of moving to the country someday. We would be like Linda and Paul McCartney, ensconced on rolling acres in the Scottish countryside, producing books and albums— venturing back to civilization once or twice a year, to receive another Grammy. Life would be simple. We would be spiritual, connected to the earth, basking in sunlight and love. But in San Francisco, because of the length of the commute to affordable land, the notion of "country" was not a real possibility.

Then we decided to move to Nashville, and suddenly, living in the country was an option. The sale of our little Mill Valley cottage produced enough income to buy the acreage we had fantasized about. Rolling hills, ponds, grassy meadows. Not only could we afford it monetarily, but in Nashville, the "country" can be as close as twenty minutes to downtown. We could stay connected to our urban lifeline while returning each eve to our country home.

The real-estate agent took us through a picture book of possibilities beyond our wildest dreams. Ten acres here, twenty there. Ponds. Corrals. We picked a place that had it all, and buckled our seat belts for the ride out of town toward what we knew was to be our destiny.

Maybe if it hadn't just rained. You see, the driveway in—which looked to our untrained eyes like a country road—had turned to mud. No problem, the real-estate agent said gamely, as she dug her sedan out of a tarry ditch. All it needed was a little gravel. A half-mile of gravel, we calculated, as the tires finally found solid ground and rolled toward our country home. Past the pond. The pond was big and round, just like they showed in the picture. But it was covered with an odoriferous green slime, and dead fish were floating on the top. No problem, the agent offered. They must have let the pH balance get out of whack. A little dredging, some chemicals. She even knew the name of a great fish hatchery that could restock it. But from that point on, nothing appeared to us at face value. The acres and acres of rolling lawn: It would need mowing. And not just once, but week after week. (Buy a tractor?) And the splendid stand of corn—watch out for rattlesnakes.

It's not that the place wasn't incredible—just right for somebody who had even the slightest notion of what living in the country truly entails—it's just that it wasn't our dream. Our dream made no mention of pH balance.

"Let me show you this other listing. I know it will be perfect!" the agent said.

But we realized that no listing in the country would be perfect for us, for we had forgotten that fifteen acres of countryside is also fifteen acres of responsibility. Assessing our own capabilities and resources, and making the necessary compromises with our dreams, we settled for one suburban acre closer into town. It's more park than country, but it delivers far more of the experience we had been hoping for out of this move than what our fantasies could have ever delivered.

Every life bears with it a rent that must be paid. Before you invest too much in something you're sure will make your life perfect, make sure it will be worth the price you're going to have to pay.

38

Indulge Your Emotions

There is sometimes a very thin line between being honest and wallowing. You are being honest if feelings of remorse and self-criticism are identifiable, and lead you toward rectification. You may well be tending toward the self-indulgent if your negative emotions are amorphous, leading to lethargy rather than action. You know the kind of pervasive, ill-defined mood I'm talking about. You walk into your workplace, and you don't like anyone or anything. Yesterday, everything was fine. But today, you and your life are hopeless and useless. Or you look in the mirror and see only your flaws, feeling yourself to be a failed human being living a meaningless life.

The general rule of thumb at such a moment is simply this:

Don't take yourself seriously. If there's something you specifically don't like about yourself or your situation, fine. Do everything you can to change it. But if it's everything about you and your life, consider the possibility that you aren't seeing things clearly right now. You are, in fact, indulging your emotions.

But before you criticize yourself even further by adding self-indulgence to your already formidable list of failings, consider that given what your disappointment has cost you, it's perfectly normal and natural to want an abundance of something in your life right now. If the only abundance you have readily available to you at this moment is self-pity and self-criticism, so be it. Don't fight it. Go with it. Indulge your emotions and they will soon, of their own accord, exhaust themselves.

The first time I realized this was on a sunny summer day several years ago. My family and I had plans to spend the afternoon at a local swim club's pool. But first, I had to see one of our clients for a monthly meeting. Because this was a routine session, I didn't think much about it. Until I got there and he told me that this was to be our last meeting. We were fired. Consumed with anger, self-pity, and remorse, I finally made it to the club. But I was in no mood for frolicking. The sun may have been shining, but I was shrouded in darkness. Somewhere, outside the fog that surrounded me, I could hear my children's cheery shouts and splashing water, but I was never going to be happy again. Dan begged me to come in, but I refused, knuckles gripped tightly on the arms of my chaise longue. The kids invited and cajoled. But I would not be budged. Finally, Dan suggested that I could at least move to the edge of the hot tub. I love hot tubs.

"You can bring your bad mood with you," he suggested, promising to respect the sanctity of my desolation.

"I can bring it with me?"

"Promise."

So, reluctantly, I dangled my feet in the swirling water. It felt good. Before long, one of my kids came by and gave a little splash. I gave a little splash back. Before I knew it, I was engaged in a water fight of monumental proportions. Even as I clutched on to my unhappiness as tightly as I could, the hot, bubbly water drowned it. While there were real implications to having been fired that I would have to confront at some point, they could hold their own until regular office hours. And I, having injected some vitality back into my spirit, would be in better shape to deal with them than had I resisted the invitation to bring my bad mood to the party. I realized something that day that I've never forgotten. Nobody says you can't be in a bad mood and in the hot tub all at the same time.

39

Think About Somebody Else's Problems

The wealthy youth came to the Zen master to solve his problem. Spoiled and pampered, the boy had no capacity to stick with things. He asked the master the key to enlightenment that would allow him to make something of himself.

The master looked him over, seeing soft, unlined hands and rich silk robes. "Tell me something you love to do," the master finally inquired.

"There is only one thing," the boy replied. "I love to play chess."

"Good," the master said. "Then we will play chess. But there's one stipulation. You must be willing to play by my rules."

The youth was so desperate, he agreed. The two sat down to play.

"So," said the master. "There's only one new rule. Whoever loses must die."

The youth began to sweat profusely. What had he gotten himself into? He looked at the master to see if this was a joke, but the master was busy studying the board. The youth hesitated, but finally, the master said, "Your move."

The boy never concentrated so hard on anything in his life. With his life at stake, he saw many moves ahead. He was brilliant in his strategies. Piece by piece, he gained the upper hand. Now he watched in horror as the old master made a fatal blunder. The boy looked up at the master, who continued to concentrate on the board as if oblivious to his mistake. The boy took in the master's wise old eyes, his wrinkled hands. The master, who had helped so many, sat across from the youth, who had dealt his life away in useless idylls. And then it was decided. The boy moved a useless pawn, leaving the master's king untouched. At that moment, the master suddenly stood up, overturning the board. All the pieces went flying.

"Today, nobody shall die," the master exclaimed. "You have attained your greatest desire. Not only have you discovered your great capacity to concentrate—but even more importantly, you have demonstrated your great capacity for compassion. These are all that are needed to live a great and important life."

40

Entertain the Kindness of Strangers

*"Ah done been in sorrow's kitchen and ah licked de
pots clean."*

—GULLAH WOMAN'S PROVERB

At this very moment, as alone and isolated as you may feel, you have, in fact, joined ranks with hundreds, thousands, or even billions of people who are dealing with pain very much like your own. You have been laid off from your job? So, today, were forty thousand people laid off from a single multinational corporation. Your test results came back with upsetting results? What are the statistics of people who have shared this exact same disappointment? One in three? Seventy percent of the adult population? You have been disappointed in love? How many people around the world at this exact moment are nursing a broken heart?

I know you never thought that this would happen to you. The fact that it has happened to one or to four billion others does not minimize the cutting edge of legitimate pain you are experiencing. What it does do is put you into the company of others who are uniquely prepared to understand what you are going through.

Some of these people have had some time—and maybe even some healing—around the very same issues your pain has brought to the surface of your life. Perhaps they have already formed a support group in your community, or on the Internet, that you can tap into for information, understanding, and companionship. Sometimes it is easier to share your feelings with an anonymous group of strangers than it is with the people in your life who have a vested interest in your happiness. This is natural and normal. Many newspapers have listings of such groups. If you do some research, you will probably uncover a group or site dedicated to the very issues your situation raises for you.

Consider, too, that some of those individuals who have suffered a disappointment such as yours are also just now coming to grips with the implications of their situation. Because of the life experience you have to share, consider what wisdom or information or compassion you have to share with others facing similar challenges.

41

Consider the Consequences

There was once a Sufi whose disappointment in life was no greater and no less than anyone else's. But so focused was he on his own life and problems, this particular man did not know that this was the case. He truly believed himself to be the most beleaguered of souls in all the world.

And so, it came about naturally that he decided to devote his life to finding the solution to his problems. Because he lived in a small town built around a village green, soon everyone in the town knew about his great suffering. Every day he would come to the square, hoping to find relief. Over and over again he told his sad story, as he searched the eager, interested faces that gathered about him for answers. They nodded and wept. Some touched his arm

softly and others brought him homemade soup. But still his problems persisted.

Perhaps there is no one in this village who can truly understand the nature of my suffering, the man thought. And so it was,
he sadly bid them farewell and set out into the unknown in search
of the solution to his problems.

Traveling alone, with only a bag of clothes over his shoulder, he
wandered for days, months, and then years. A tragic figure of a
magnitude achieved by few, his fame soon began to spread
throughout the kingdom. Everywhere he went, he told his sad
story. Touched by his tale of woe, strangers lent him donkeys to
ride and spare rooms in which to sleep. Women sought to give him
comfort and hope. Children brought him little homemade presents
to cheer him up. But still, no one could offer him the resolution he
sought.

For years and years, the man—now very old—continued his
search for answers. As he looked, he met many people and had
many great adventures. Yet no one could help him, and so he kept
on.

Until one day he came to the outskirts of a village unlike any
he had ever seen before. This village was surrounded by a warm
white mist. The homes in this village were not made of brick and
mud, but of finespun gossamer and gold. Eagerly, he looked
around to find someone to ask the name of this extraordinary
place—but there was nobody to be found. Then, suddenly, he saw
a shaft of light open up from the very heavens, shining directly
upon the doorway of the grandest home in the village. Following
the beam of light, he approached the large golden door and pre-

pared to knock. But just as he raised his fist, he saw that there was a notice etched into the shiny metal. The Solutions You've Been Seeking, the words read.

The man hesitated for a long moment, staring at the words he had been trying to find all his life. Then he looked behind him at the long road from whence he had come. Then, quietly, he bent down to remove his shoes and tiptoed away as quickly as he could.

42

Tell the Whole Truth

You believe that all is lost—but is it possible that you have merely released that which has served its purpose so that your life may proceed unhampered by structures you have already outgrown?

You have said that you are inadequate—but is it possible that you have set high standards for yourself, to stretch you beyond that to which you would not otherwise have aspired?

You bemoan that you were overlooked—but is it possible that you are being left to ripen on the vine to be plucked when you will be the sweetest of all?

43

Get Used to Dust

Many of us feel that no matter how much we accomplish, it's never going to be enough. We understand all too well a John Quincy Adams, who near the end of his life was quoted as saying, "My life has been spent in vain aspirations." Or Robert Louis Stevenson, who proposed this inscription for his tombstone: "Here lies one who meant well."

While I have a tendency to feel this way about myself, early on in my writing career, I received a great gift from somebody I will always remember fondly. Her name was Erma Bombeck, sent by *Good Morning America* to do a piece on my ideas about finding balance between work and relaxation. Her crew was to film me in one of my favorite pastimes, rowing on San Francisco Bay. She came to the door, dressed in a scrubby sweatshirt and jeans, and took one look at me, knowing she had her work cut out for her. "Is that what you wear when you row?" Knowing that this was going to air on national television, I had bought a sharp new jumpsuit, complete with gold buttons and matching earrings. "No," I admitted, "but this is how I go rowing when I'm on national television."

Erma's down-to-earth presence in the midst of my fifteen minutes of fame made a big impression on me. Over the years, we kept in touch. Her message to me was always the same: Your ordinary self is enough.

Relax, pay attention to what's real and true for you, and don't let yourself get swept up in other people's agendas for you, or your own images of what success should or ought to look like.

When I heard not so long ago that Erma had passed away, I grieved for the loss of somebody special not only to me, but to much of the world. But in the midst of my sorrow, I suddenly remembered something about Erma that made me laugh out loud. I remembered what she had once said she hoped to have written on her tombstone. Those of us who aspire to greatness, who try hard to make our mark, who are always too hard on ourselves, heed Erma's ultimate wisdom. Her proposed tombstone epitaph?

"BIG DEAL. I'M USED TO DUST."

44

Trade in Your Sack of Troubles

*M*y grandmother once took me to see a wonderful old friend who told me a Yiddish folktale from his childhood. The story is about a villager, who once complained incessantly about his lot in life. Over and over, he would look at his neighbors, each of whom appeared more fortunate than he, wishing that he could trade his life for theirs. Finally, after many years, the man was visited by an angel who came to grant him his fondest wish.

"Gather all your troubles into a sack and bring them to the outskirts of the village. There you will be free to trade in your sack for any bag of troubles in the pile," the angel promised.

Cheered at last by the hope of a rosier future, the villager hurried along, carrying his great sack of problems. Every step of the way, the man's sack seemed to feel heavier and heavier. At last, the weight became so great, he could barely advance. But the anticipation of soon being able to trade in his sack for another, assuredly less burdensome than his own, kept his feet moving one before the other. As he trudged slowly down the dirt road, he thought of the butcher, with his big house and his lovely bride. He thought of the traveling storyteller, whose freedom to come and go as he wished was surpassed by none. He thought of the village elder whose wisdom and power had surely eliminated the mundane disappointments of daily living.

As the villager arrived, the angel relieved him of his burden and threw it into the great pile of sacks, gathered from everyone the poor man had ever envied. The angel then instructed him to take as much time as he would like, selecting in exchange whichever sack he wished to bring home with him in trade. The villager rushed to the mountain of sacks and began lifting and judging the weight and size of each one. For one day and one night, he raised and pinched, squeezed and rolled. He was determined to seek out the lightest burden in the pile.

Partway through the second day, the villager found it. There was no doubt in his mind. It was so much smaller and loosely packed than all the rest. He was certain that he had found the lightest burden of all. The angel, standing by, smiled broadly as the villager showed him the sack of troubles of his choice and returned home with it.

The sack was so light, it felt to the man as though it were filled with air. He juggled it, danced with it, and bounced it along like a ball all the way home. Then, at long last, with great anticipation, he threw it open to see whose contents he had taken in exchange for his own. Would it be the butcher's? The storyteller's? He opened the sack and peered inside.

The terrible truth dawned on him. He had chosen his own sack of troubles from the mountain of disappointments. He had judged his own sack to be the lightest and least burdensome of all.

He lived out the rest of his days accepting as his portion the limitations, disappointments, troubles, and anxieties that he had tried to trade away. He never again complained.

Unfinished Business

"If a man goes on quietly and perseveringly
working at the removal of resistance, success
comes in the end."

—THE I CHING

There comes a time when the moment has come to stop thinking and start doing. Now is the time to rectify any part you may have played in what has transpired: Get involved in the situation you've been avoiding; sacrifice your own comfort to right the wrongs. Your body and soul beg you to remove the blockages and let your spirit flow again. The very moment you begin making choices with integrity is the moment that true healing begins. From that instant on, although external outcomes may continue to unfold as the consequences of what has been set in motion, inner failures are somehow mitigated. Responding to the need deep in your soul, every step forward will be an occasion to rejoice.

45

Value the Unexpected

An eleventh-century Dervish parable teaches that sometimes what you and others think will be best for you is actually very different from what will truly serve you. In this story, a scavenger has taken up his trade in the street of perfume sellers. Attracted to the potpourri of sweet fragrances that wafted out of the shops and into the street, he thought that he had found the path to happiness.

But one day, as he was walking along doing his work, he suddenly collapsed. The shop owners came running to revive him. They held sweet fragrances beneath his nose, but the more they tried, the worse he became.

Finally, another scavenger happened by. Witnessing the collapsed fellow, he knew immediately what must be done. He searched for something filthy to place beneath the scavenger's nose, replacing the shopkeepers' perfumes with the foul-smelling mixture. Immediately, the scavenger revived.

46

Eat Your Mistake

During World War II, the mother and her young son depended on ration stamps to purchase food and other necessities while her husband was off at war. There came a time when the ration stamps were particularly scarce. Nevertheless, the mother chose to treat her son to the sweet of his choice. Surveying the possibilities, he finally made his selection. "Are you sure?" he was asked. Nodding assent, he grasped the chocolate bar firmly in his hand. She traded it for the stamp and they began the long walk home.

The first bite or two of pure chocolate were heavenly, but then the child bit into something he hadn't expected: a chewy center. He demanded that his mother take him back to the store and buy him something else. "I made a mistake, Mommy. Please let me trade it for something else." But she had neither the ration stamps nor the means to comply. And so, while it saddened her to see him so disappointed, she offered him her best advice: "Eat your mistake."

There are times in life when we must all eat our mistakes. It won't help to pitch a hissy fit if you don't happen to be holding the ration stamp that will make things perfect. You can thrash about in victimhood or self-blame, lose yourself in remorse over what could have been, or you can just simply eat the candy with the chewy center with all the dignity you can muster, and get whatever you can out of the situation you are in. Regardless of the circumstances that you are facing in your life, dignity is something that nobody can ever take from you.

47

Deal With It

You have thought through the ramifications of your disappointment, the part you played in it, why it happened, what good may come of it. You have nursed your wounds, rebuilt your foundation on more solid ground, reached out to others for comfort and help, and placed your disappointment into its greater context.

So the question before you right now is simply this: What are you going to *do* about it?

There comes a time when you must stop thinking and start doing. While it is true that the unexamined life is not a life worth living, as the folk saying goes, "The overexamined life is not a life at all."

You may prefer to mull and fiddle and pray in an endless

search for life's meaning. But is this pull to continue your contemplation driven by the desire to dive back into the heart of your life—or by the fearful attempt to protect yourself from the consequences of taking action?

If it is the latter, Ralph Waldo Emerson has this wisdom for you: "He has not learned the lesson of life who does not every day surmount a fear."

So, if all that you've felt, thought about, and talked about has not brought you the relief from your disappointment for which you've hoped, perhaps the time has come at last to take action. Assuming that you have already gathered sufficient information upon which to make informed decisions, that you have networked your options and resources, and that you have been honest about both the situation you are facing and the role that you have played in it (and even if you haven't done these things perfectly), you are now ready to take care of your unfinished business.

If dealing with the ramifications of your disappointment still seems overwhelming to you, here's a secret that might help you along. There are only two things to do:

1. Change what you can.
2. Accept what you can't.

Granted, it is not always easy to know in any given situation just what it is you should and can change and what it is you must accept. But chances are that at this point, you are equipped to make your best guess.

Of course, it is scary to take action. It's true that you might make a mistake. You might resign an unpleasant situation thinking it's hopeless only to discover that it would have turned out fine. You might decide to stay and give it a go, thinking you've got what it takes to make it turn out right, and discover that you've simply wasted your time. You might reach out to someone, hoping to make amends, and be brutally rebuffed. . . .

We give great lip service to the idea of taking risks in our society. But most of us only put ourselves out on the edge if we know that it's all going to work out. But the irony is, if you knew it was truly going to work out for you, it wouldn't be a risk.

No, recovering from disappointment, picking up the pieces, and moving on again is by its very nature a risky business. That is why Scott Peck tells his lecture audiences that the true measure of psychological health is just how many crises we can fit into the span of a lifetime.

How many crises? Of course, what Peck and Emerson are telling us is that we cannot be fully successful unless we are first fully alive. The longer you play it safe, the greater the weight your disappointment will impose upon your spirit. There comes a time when you've got to get the energy moving again.

One who engaged rather than avoided his fear was Colonel Sanders, who, in 1956, discovered that a federal highway was slated to be built soon, bypassing his roadside diner and inn. His competitors either stayed put, out of naïveté or denial (and went out of business), or threw their arms up in dismay and quit. Sanders, however, at age sixty-six, took his fried-chicken process and recipes on the road to see if he could encourage existing diners to make use of them for a fee. The rest is history.

Whether your disappointment spawns a multibillion-dollar chicken franchise or a single letter of apology or complaint, it is your challenge to respond to it fully—even if, or perhaps even especially if, such a response brings you face-to-face with fear.

48

Confess Your Shortcomings to an Empty Shower Stall

There are some among you who have a burdensome secret. For while you were sifting through the wreckage of your misfortune, you recognized bits and pieces of your own integrity scattered about. Even though others may overlook the evidence, you know it's there.

You feel guilty. You feel ashamed.

Your friends, your self-help books, even your therapist, may be urging you to extend to yourself compassion and understanding. It wasn't your fault, they comfort you. It was the way you were raised, the circumstances you faced, your genes, the economic and familial factors that pressed themselves hard upon you.

But while all this may be true, you quietly, inwardly know that you bear moral responsibility for the part you played: actions that hurt or damaged others or even yourself.

What should you do?

You should make amends. Rectify what you can. Stop keeping your terrible secret and share your intention to make things right again with the people who ought to know about your part in it. Write that difficult letter. Fix what you broke. Sacrifice your own comfort to right the wrong in which you participated. Get involved in the situation you have been avoiding.

Above all, be grateful for your guilt. This uncomfortable mental and emotional state is giving you the opportunity to realize that no matter how brilliant your rationalizations, even you aren't buying them. Not only are you admitting that you're troubled, but you confess that aspects of what you did were wrong. You stand at last on the solid ground of the truth, willing to face things as they really are.

Obstacles like unhandled guilt and shame are like a dam in your spirit, blocking your creative energy and preventing you from moving on in your life. Our bodies and souls beg us to remove the blockages and let the spirit flow again.

But what if there's no one to make amends to—nothing you can do to right the wrong you have done? Joan Borysenko, Ph.D., cites studies that show that individuals can achieve relief from their shame and guilt by confessing out loud, even if they direct their repentance to a shower curtain with no one behind it. If confessing to a shower curtain has positive results, how much more effective it would be right now to connect with the traditions of confession and repentance embodied by your spiritual or religious tradition.

"It is dangerous to perform surgery on the soul," the great rabbi from Lublin known as the Kotzker wrote in the early 1800s. But people "must live dangerously."

49

Spend Quality Time With Someone Worse Off Than You

Do you still think you've got the biggest problem in the world? Now, it is possible that not only are you upset about what has happened to you, but also about the part you may have played in it. Perhaps you are kicking and screaming about how miserable a human being you are. Nobody has ever been so lost and so mistaken. You are wallowing in the underbelly of your emotions, absolutely certain of your special status.

And there's a name for this common malady. It's called grandiosity. Grandiosity, which afflicts each of us from time to time, is the larger-than-life notion that the world centers on you and your problems as being more important, more terrible, more painful than whatever happens to be occurring to anyone else anywhere in the world.

Fortunately, there's a cure. Call or visit somebody you know who makes your mountain of problems look like a hill of beans. This is a good time, for instance, to call your whining cousin whose life is always in a state of disarray.

Or better yet, you could take the high road to humility while doing some good for the community along the way. Volunteer your time at a local homeless or hospice shelter. Hospitals, retirement homes, youth centers are always in need of an extra pair of helping hands. It will probably be a great relief to you to be thinking about somebody else's problems for a change.

50

All You Can Do

"It is only when we have the courage to face things exactly as they are, without any sort of self-deception or illusion, that a light will develop out of events, by which the path to success may be recognized."

—THE I CHING

Sometimes it feels as if the path to rectification and recovery leads not toward the light, but rather into a bottomless void of darkness. We feel overwhelmed by our limitations and shortcomings. Where can one begin?

In his book *Disciplines of the Spirit*, theologian Howard Thurman teaches us that regardless of the errors we have made, the very moment we begin making choices with integrity is the very moment that our recovery begins. From that moment on, although external results may continue to unfold as the ruthless consequences of what has been set in motion by the wrong act, "the inner failure is somehow mitigated."

You restore your integrity when you sincerely make amends, praying for restoration not as a child, stamping your foot in petulance, crying out, "Here is my authentic self. I have done my part. Now you have to love and forgive me."

Rather, innocence begins when you expose your broken heart, in all sadness and humility, saying, "Here is my authentic self, flaws and all. While I prefer that you love and forgive me, I accept whatever the consequences may be."

This is the beginning of true prayer.

51

Counteract Your Tendencies

The elderly, frail rabbi felt compelled to undertake a perilous journey in order to do a good deed in the mountainous terrain beyond the gates of his village. He journeyed for many days and at last approached his destination, a shepherd's hut in which an old friend lay dying. But between himself and the hut stretched a seemingly bottomless chasm. The rains had washed away the simple bridge the shepherd's family once so joyously traversed. And so, the rabbi asked God what to do. Immediately, his eyes fell upon the trunk of a fallen tree. While it would easily stretch across the chasm, it was very narrow and unstable. With great effort, the rabbi managed to swing the log into place, securing it as best he could. Praying that it would hold, he inched his way forward step by step, finally making it across to the little hut. And after he had done his good deed, he made it back again in the same manner.

When he returned to his village, he told his students about what had transpired.

"Rabbi," one asked. "The bridge was so unsteady. How could you ever have made it across that chasm?"

"How did I manage?" the rabbi replied. "Simply this. When I felt myself toppling to one side, I leaned to the other."

So it is with your own journey. You can progress toward recovery simply by counteracting your excesses. If you have a tendency to say no, try saying yes. If you lean always toward compliance, balance your tendency with resistance. If you have been passive, try taking action. If you tend to blame yourself for things, seek to recognize those aspects for which you bear no responsibility. If you have been in a frenzy, try calming down.

Get the balance right with yourself, and you, too, will reach your goal.

52

Ride a Roller Coaster

When you are ready to let your disappointment go, take it for a roller coaster ride. You know the kind of roller coaster I'm talking about. The kind that climbs into the sky, then dives into the depths, a few brave individuals throwing their arms up over their heads on the descent—everybody screaming.

As you make the first big climb, imagine all the time, energy, and emotion you've already invested in your misfortune. Really feel the pain. You don't need to do this anymore. It's time to let it go. You know it. I know it. So, as you reach the peak of the climb, say good-bye to it. Scream good-bye to it—then be one of the brave ones.

As you rush into the descent, throw your arms up over your head and leave your pain behind.

53

Laugh Into the Mirror

*E*veryone has family stories. My favorite story about my father goes back to World War II, when he was a physician stationed in the Philippines. As part of the medical corps, he was soon sent to the front lines to handle the casualties that came about, both from battle and from the tropical diseases that abounded. But before long, he himself succumbed to a fever. He was helped by the other medical personnel to a cot in the medic tent, where his illness raged on. But soon, the medical corps received orders to clear out. The enemy was advancing and they were ordered to move to a new position in great haste. The medics rapidly dismantled the tent, overwhelmed by the patients and supplies. Somehow, they got the Jeeps packed and made their hasty retreat.

There was one thing. In the panic of the moment, they had

forgotten my father, lying on the cot, feverish, ill, and alone in the middle of an empty field. As my father's dilemma dawned on him, he recognized the tenuousness of his situation. In the distance, he could hear gunfire. Too weak to get up, he pondered his choices.

He could scream, cry, or panic. But all alone in the middle of a vast field, what good would that do? He could be angry with himself for getting into this jam—or better yet, turn against those who had left him behind so thoughtlessly. But if these moments were truly to be his last, was that how he wanted his life to go? Suddenly, out of some secret depths, he found the answer. What was the best response given the dire circumstances he faced? He started to laugh.

Whether it was the delirium or enlightenment, he saw the humor in his situation—and in the human condition, overall. In an instant, he forgave himself and forgave those who had abandoned him. He lay on the cot and laughed and laughed and laughed.

Before too long, his fellow medics realized, in great horror, their terrible mistake. Risking their lives, they rushed back to the field, dodging the gunfire, and carried my father back out of harm's way.

Even now, fifty years later, my father's choice—made on that sweat-soaked cot in the midst of the enemy's battlefield—continues to reverberate through his life, and through all the lives he has touched. He continues to laugh at fate's twists and turns, preferring to assign irony rather than blame when things don't go his way. He sees everything that there is to be seen, and yet he chooses to let many things pass. He is quick to smile and quick to forgive.

Try it yourself. Walk over to a mirror right now. Look deep into your eyes and give a deep, great belly laugh. Do this every morning. Make it a habit—for life.

54

Bless Their Hearts

Sometimes you are blessed with the spontaneous ability to forgive others for the pain they have caused you. All of a sudden, you see that given who they are, where they came from, and the forces they were up against, they were doing the best they could. That does not mean that you necessarily choose to stay in a relationship with them—but at least you have compassion and understanding for them.

But there are times when you quite simply cannot just skip over the anger and resentment you are feeling and go all the way to compassion and absolution.

When I lived in the Bay Area, I searched for the key to forgiveness. From my spiritual studies, I learned how to meditate in order to transcend my anger. I was taught how to use my breath to transform negative energy into love. I performed rituals of forgiveness, releasing my resentments—writ large on brightly colored paper—to the flames of a burning log.

But even so, there were those people and those times when I could not let my resentment go.

Then I moved to the South. And was exposed to a new way of life by the likes of TV star Dixie Carter; I learned a method that, of all the many technologies I have mastered, I have found to be most consistently useful. It comes not from contemporary psychological theory or advanced stages of spiritual mastery. It comes, instead, from the tried-and-true tradition of good Southern manners.

So here's what the Southerners taught me.

You can say whatever it is you want about somebody—just as long as you tack "Bless her heart" at the end of it.

"She certainly knows how to put her own needs first, bless her heart."

"He has more than a few screws loose, bless his heart."

"He drinks like a fish, bless his heart."

Go ahead and meditate, perform your rituals of absolution. But in the meantime, while you're waiting for forgiveness to kick in, know that you've got the right to feel every single one of your nasty little emotions. Offer your enemies a blessing, even if offered Southern style, and you just might discover that you really do have the potential to forgive just about anyone, bless your heart.

55

Remember That You Are Loved

"God does not want us to be burdened because of sorrows and tempests that happen in our lives, because it has always been so before miracles happen."

—JULIAN OF NORWICH

The fourteenth-century Christian mystic Julian of Norwich lived in England during a time of famine, plague, and poverty. While the religious establishment attributed the people's misfortune to a punishing God issuing judgment on their sins, Julian envisioned a compassionate God who felt reverence for each and every one of us. Here is a meditation for you, based on her writings.

Remembering

I admit that I am often discouraged by the news that reaches my ears—and by the painful things that have happened to me, as well. Nevertheless, I have compassion for myself, understanding that my shaky faith is not derived from any willful intention on my part, but rather because I am so prone to forget that I am loved by God always.

I forget and remember and forget over and over again. And yet, God, you embrace me with compassion, saying to me:

Do not accuse yourself too much, allowing your troubles to seem all your fault. It is not my will that you bear your toils and pains heavily. For when you allow yourself to be borne down by your shortcomings, you are not able to see your God's joyful face, not at all!

I love you. I never began to love you. I have known and loved you from without beginning. I know that your shortcomings fall to you against your will—and so it is that you must trust even this: Your darkest and bitterest failings are under my care.

I am your friend who keeps you tenderly when you have failed, showing you where you went wrong by the sweet

light of compassion and grace, even though you imagine
that you will be punished.

God, you did not say: You will not labor hard; you will
not be troubled. But you did say: *You will not be over-*
come. God, help me to take your promises as much as
my capabilities allow. This is your will.

This prayer is based on an interpretation of Julian of Norwich's writing by Doyle Brendan.

56

Build Anew

The rabbi of Berditchev teaches that one who is truly joyful is like a man whose house has burned down. Unlike those who entertain themselves with empty pleasure, devoid of inner substance, his need is deep in his soul. When he begins to build anew, every stone laid is an occasion to rejoice.

Uncharted Territory

"If we let things terrify us, life will not be worth living."

—SENECA

After you have forgiven others, mourned your losses, salvaged the best possible outcome, you have done enough about the past. Now is the time to leave the charted waters of your misfortune, setting out through treacherous seas to ports unknown. While it is true that you can influence your fate, you cannot control it. No matter how hard you try, how smart or wise you are, your life will spin out of your control from time to time. The risk is great. But if you hope to master the art of resilience, quite simply, you have no choice. You must allow yourself to respond to the urge calling you beyond the familiar and into the unexplored territory of fresh vision where the questions are as important as the answers.

57

Set Sail for Open Waters

There comes a time when you have done what has been called for. You have rectified things to the best of your ability, forgiven others, mourned your losses, salvaged the best possible outcome. You have done enough. And yet, there is the temptation to keep your disappointment close to you. Over and over again, you take it out and gaze upon it with morbid fascination. *What could I have done differently? If only . . . What if . . . How could I have . . .* You know it is time to release your disappointment and move on, and yet you continue to cling. Why?

Because on some level, you realize that the moment you admit that you have done enough, you will be free to look forward rather than back. But what will you see? The landscape of your life has been changed by what has happened. Before you lies uncharted territory. Certain options and possibilities you once thought you had open to you have been closed off, while other routes, leading into the unknown, begin to emerge from the mist. *What if I pick the wrong one? Where will it lead? What if I end up disappointed again?*

The future is frightening to think about. It's easier to rerun the past over and over again, looking for places where you can shore up the breaches in hopes of a better outcome next time. *If only I had done better, not missed the opportunity, worked smarter.* In your quest for mastery, you find it preferable to keep working the past over rather than confronting the truth. But the truth presses in upon you, like water breaching a dam. The memory of your disappointment, the place where it hurts most, is the exact place where the truth will break through.

And what is the truth? Life does not always meet your standards. You cannot always get things to turn out for you just the way you want. You are not always protected from pain. Life is not always fair.

To admit to these truths, and yet to retain faith and hope that life may yet reclaim a sense of meaning, requires courage. It will take compassion and patience.

You can accomplish this; you will, however, have to leave the charted waters of your disappointment, setting out in your tiny boat through treacherous seas to ports unknown. In our own ways, each of us who becomes willing to engage the truth becomes an adventurer. Thor Heyerdahl, who some years ago re-created the voyage he believed the Egyptians to have made across the Atlantic Ocean to South America, provides us with inspiration for our journey. Setting forth in his primitive boat, the *Kon-Tiki*, he noted that all the dangers lay close to the shore. Once one has broken through the shoals and reefs, the expanse of ocean brings great relief.

So it is in your life. When you attempt to hang on to the past, you are in the greatest peril. The future is uncharted territory—but it is where hope lies. There are no guarantees. The risk is great. But if you want to be fully alive, quite simply, you have no choice.

58

Go Wild

Once upon a time, there was a little white rabbit named Gregory. Gregory lived in a safe, warm room in the back of a thatched cottage with his master, a gentle man with big, strong hands that stroked his fur and made sure his bowl was always full of good, fresh orange and green things to eat.

But there came a day when his master went away and never returned. When first the food was gone, and then the water, Gregory realized that he was going to need help. He began to dig at the dirt floor beside the front door, looking for a way out. As the hunger and thirst churned his stomach, he dug more and more frantically until, at last, he tunneled his way outside.

As he looked around, he soon realized that he had no idea

where to begin. He didn't even know what a carrot growing in the ground looked like! And then there were the wild things, scary animals with yellow eyes, whom he'd heard calling in the night as he sat by his warm fire—and who, he realized with a sickening feeling in the pit of his stomach, would find him to be a tasty morsel, indeed. Despairing, Gregory lay down on the edge of the forest, just behind the empty cottage, and began to sob loudly.

"Well, well, well." Gregory sat bolt upright as the confident voice of a huge wild brown rabbit broke through his sobs.

"I've lost my master," Gregory cried. "And now I will surely die of starvation, or get swallowed by something horrible."

"I see," the wild rabbit replied. "And this is why you cry?"

"What else would I be crying about?" Gregory answered.

"We all thought you were overcome with joy," he replied. "For years, we pressed our noses against the window of your cottage at night, as you sat by the fire, and felt so sorry for you."

"Sorry for me?"

"Trapped all alone in that overheated cage of a cottage. No freedom. No adventure. No rabbits to keep you company. I'm glad to see you bust loose at last. I'll show you the ropes, if you'd like."

"The ropes? But you don't expect me to actually live out here—live wild, like you. Who will bring me my dinner?"

"You are crying because you no longer live in a safe world," said the big brown rabbit. "But don't you see? The truth is, it never was. Your comfort depended solely on your master's caretaking. But we wild animals have never had any of your comforts. And yet we've lived every day of our lives, same as you. We don't know what tomorrow may bring—maybe a wild dog will come and eat us for dinner. But that's no more dangerous than what happened to you. Since there's no safety anywhere, you might as well stop crying and start living."

Gregory listened to the brown rabbit's words, his teary eyes drifting back to the cottage where he had spent so many peaceful days. If what the rabbit was saying was true, there would be pain and risk no matter what he chose to do. Every fiber of his being was urging him to stay put, to wait for his master to return. But even if he did, what would prevent his master from leaving again? Gregory sat quietly for many moments. He sighed deeply. He looked at the empty cottage. He looked at the woods beyond the field. He looked back at the cottage. He looked at the rabbit. And then suddenly, kicking up great clouds of straw with their furry paws, two wild rabbits exuberantly hopped off and away to search for supper.

59

Try to Stop the Waves
From Rolling In

While it is true that you can influence your fate, you cannot control it. No matter how hard you try, how good your intentions, how smart or wise you are, your life will spin out of your control from time to time.

Of course you wish you could guarantee the outcomes you want each and every time, but beware of spiritual and philosophical end runs around these truths that may give you the illusion of short-term mastery but will fail you when you need them most.

As Sandy, a respected person in our community, lay dying of breast cancer in a local hospital, a mutual friend came to me in tears. While she had been visiting with Sandy, praying for God to release Sandy from her devastating pain as quickly as possible, a young chaplain had come to call. He instructed the visitors in the room to hold hands and exhorted Sandy to purify her heart and throw off the illness. "If only you and we believe strongly enough, God will respond with a miracle, and Sandy may yet be healed," he said.

Fervently, they clutched hands and prayed, but Sandy's condition worsened rather than improved and soon the intensive-care nurse ushered them out. My friend was racked with guilt and shame. Had she not believed strongly enough? Was her heart not pure enough? Was it Sandy's lack of faith? When Sandy died the next day, my friend began the serious work of embarking on a new worldview large enough to contain even this painful experience—and anything else that might come her way over the years. She knew she needed to find some way of living in an unpredictable world that could be counted on to embrace her and those she cared about with compassion and faith whether things turned out the way she wanted—or not.

Thankfully, she found a book in a used-book store that helped her begin to separate the superficial from real spirituality. The book was by J. Macmurry, author of *Persons in Relation:*

> The maxim of illusory religion runs: "Fear not; trust in God and He will see that none of the things you fear will happen to you"; that of real religion, on the contrary, is "Fear not: The things that you are afraid of are quite likely to happen to you, but they are nothing to be afraid of."

Macmurry understands what the young chaplain did not: that when you are urged to do or be anything special in order to get the divine to deliver the results you want—be pure enough, optimistic or faithful enough—you are being set up to believe that you are calling the shots. Of course you should do what you can, but remember that there are forces beyond your control. There are things we cannot know. There is mystery. So beware of spiritual formulations that offer shortcuts around ultimate truths.

Sometimes, it is helpful to have a graphic reminder that this world is quite simply not your show. One way to really get this message is to go to the nearest ocean and try to stop the waves from rolling in.

Of course, you can't succeed—and you can't succeed in keeping problems and disappointments from happening to you from time to time in your life, either.

But always remember that you can't stop the good things from happening either—and often when you least expect it.

As Helen Keller once wrote: "Life is a great adventure, or it is nothing. There is no such thing as security."

60

Escape From a
Chinese Finger Puzzle

$\mathcal{M}$y daughter's school invited me to talk about my writing. To illustrate one of my principles, I purchased a sack of Chinese finger puzzles—colorful tubes woven out of thin wooden strips.

On the day of my talk, the preteens were remarkably attentive as I described my writing process. And then it came time to hand out the puzzles, one per child.

"What lesson can you learn from the Chinese finger puzzle?" I asked them.

I asked Jody to demonstrate. She came to the front of the auditorium, placed her pointing fingers inside each end of the tube, and the class followed suit.

The solution to the puzzle is this. The harder you pull, the tighter the woven tube becomes. In order to escape from the finger trap, you must relax.

The children could not hear me, however, as I demonstrated and explained the solution. These children, having grown up far from Chinatowns of any size or shape, had never seen one of these gizmos before. And so it was that when their fingers got trapped, many of them panicked. I could hear squeals and screams. I saw wood chips flying. There were panicky eyes and a few tears.

It was pandemonium for several long minutes. And then, at last, the finger traps removed, order restored, I vowed that next time I would do the demonstration and give the explanation before handing out the puzzles—not during.

I've told this story on several occasions to groups of adults, and we have a good laugh at the children's expense. Wood chips flying, screams and all. But the truth is that most of us, when confronted with a puzzle in our own lives, do the very same thing. We panic and start to pull for all we're worth to get out of the tight spot we've stumbled into. We follow what feels to be the most reasonable, rational course, using force and will to get us out of the fix we're in. When things tighten up on us, we try even harder. And the harder we try, the worse it gets. The last thing that occurs to us is to relax. But more often than not, that is exactly the thing to do.

I now keep a Chinese finger puzzle beside my computer so that when I tighten up under pressure, I can remind myself that sometimes the fastest and best way out of trouble is not to push through—but to relax.

61

Color Outside the Lines

*"Eternity is with us, inviting our contemplation
perpetually, but we are too frightened, lazy,
and suspicious to respond: . . . It needs
industry and goodwill if we would make that
transition: for the process involves a veritable
spring-cleaning of the soul . . ."*

—Evelyn Underhill

When we do as we are told, we live in a world of superficial meanings. Coloring inside the lines, we are urged to act, perform, and consume as expected.

In this orderly, pale world—the space inside the lines—deeper meanings are drowned out by the din of commercials encouraging us to find happiness through the purchase of this or that new and improved product. Long hours at the office, required to underwrite the synthetically produced version of a successful and meaningful life, leave time enough for anxiety—but not enough for contemplation. The more tender yearnings of heart and soul, hearty as they may be to survive at all, have not the strength to push up through the concrete edifices that circumscribe the busyness that we call the successful life.

One begins to color outside the lines when one becomes willing to be a truth teller. We must take on the dangerous task of stripping away our false understandings of life and of meaning down to the barest bones. One must become willing to struggle with the big questions—to huddle naked and alone in the shadow of the mystery. One must be willing to submit one's fondest notions about how the world works to scrutiny. One must find it within one's self to sit quietly, empty, waiting for the inspiration to put crayon to paper and draw the one true line that one has been called to do.

Your disappointment is calling you to color outside the lines, recognizing, in the words of mystic Evelyn Underhill, that your "whole life is enmeshed in great and living forces; terrible because unknown." You must allow yourself to respond to the call that urges you beyond the stale aspects of your life, old habits that anesthetize your perceptions in the tepid air of familiarity—and into the unexplored territory of fresh vision.

Open the windows so that the sounds of the wild can penetrate your heart with their music of awe and wonder. Walk out into the night sky, consumed with humility at the infinite expanse of stars and planets. Feel how small we all are, and how immense the time and space within which we dance for such a brief moment. Color outside the lines.

62

Pray as You Are

There came a time when a spiritual master was to travel with his disciples to a distant city. The city boasted a spiritual center of great repute, and the master warmly anticipated his visit to the sacred gathering place.

When the master arrived, he refused to enter. His disciples asked him why he hesitated. At last, the master replied that he sensed that something was wrong.

"This place is full of prayer," the master explained.

"But what could be wrong with this?" asked the disciples, for this seemed to them to be the highest praise, providing even more encouragement to go inside.

When they pressed the question, the master explained: "Words spoken without fear cannot rise to heaven. This place is filled only with desires and certainty. The people here want only to do right in order to make themselves look good to God. We must travel on until we find a place where the people are aware of their inadequacy."

Story inspired by Rabbi Levi Yitzhak.

63

Ask the Big Questions

May a power greater than myself,

Grace me with humility so that I may set aside what I think I know in order to tremble before your awesome mystery.

Grant me the courage to test my beliefs against holocaust, injustice, and death.

Give me the strength to challenge you when I see wrongs in the world and in my life.

Make me willing to relinquish my quest for peace and love when I am called into discomfort and sacrifice.

Release me from the arrogant notion that you will accept the deals I offer on the terms of my choosing.

Stay with me when all I can say is that I don't really know the whole truth about me—and I fear the worst.

Help me to trust that even as I wrestle with the big questions, all is not in vain and that my life may yet be meaningful.

64

Give Up Needing to Know

She was already old when she met the man of her dreams. All of her life she had longed for such perfection. For five beautiful years, they lived together. Every day was a blessing, full of love and light. And then she died.

Standing before the angel who awaited her at the gate to heaven, she begged for an explanation.

"Why couldn't you have sent him to me earlier?" she cried. "When I think of how many men I tried to love, with so little in return. And then to get it all—but so late! Why did I have to wait so long?"

The angel replied.

"In your twenties, you knew exactly what you wanted out of life. You chose Mark and it didn't work out.

"When you were in your thirties and forties, you thought you knew what would make you happy. You chose Stan and it didn't work out.

"When you were in your fifties, you believed you had learned from your experiences and that now you knew what was right for you. You chose Martin and it didn't work out.

"In your sixties, you realized you didn't have a clue and gave up."

"Yes, that's true," the old woman replied. "And then after that, I met Carl and had the happiest five years of my life. But that still doesn't answer my question. Why did it take so long?"

"That's easy," replied the angel. "I was waiting for you to finish taking your turn."

65

Withhold Judgment

$\mathcal{A}$s the day unfolded, I felt increasingly good about how far I'd come as a workshop leader. When, after one particularly deep meditation, I noticed how many hands were raised for hankies to wipe away tears, I began to feel the full impact of the day I had constructed. I began to feel how powerful I had become.

But then things took a sudden turn for the worse. Not for the one hundred or so workshop attendees, but for me. For during the next section of the workshop, I noticed someone wasn't participating. The group had explicitly been told to write nonstop for ten minutes, whatever was on their minds. Pens swung into action, hankies waving, paper flying. But there, toward the back of the room, one darkly dressed woman sat immobile. The melodic piano music from the CD player drenched her in tones programmed for inspiration, but she stared vacantly into space.

Through the subsequent concluding exercises, I found myself checking on her progress. Surely, she was not beyond me. I could reach her. I would move her. But there she sat, stony-faced and silent. Was I, then, less powerful than I'd previously assumed? Was I, in fact, a failure? As the workshop ended and people came up to me to tell me how much they'd gotten from the day, I found it increasingly difficult to hold on to my indulgent self-pity. Clearly, while I could not accomplish all of my goals, I had certainly accomplished some of what I intended. I recognized, in the shattering of my personal celebration of power, the welcome relief of finding myself returned to my true size, neither larger nor smaller than who I really am.

I was about to leave for home when I noticed her sitting quietly. She stood up and approached me. "My two boys and husband were killed in a car wreck two years ago," she said. "I have not been able to be among groups of people since then. I've tried, but I've always left in the middle. Today, I stayed all the way through. I want you to know that I was here today. Thank you."

We think we understand things, what it means to be powerful, what it means to surrender control. Even as we release, we judge our progress. We move a step ahead and fall ten paces behind. We soar, we plummet. But through it all, she was here today. And so, too, was I.

66

Hold a Garage Sale

What are the old beliefs, prejudices, stresses, obligations, and behaviors that you no longer want or need? Let them go. Physically take the reminders of those things that you have outgrown and put them in a garage-sale pile.

What is it that reminds you of the biggest behavior or belief that you are still carrying with you that you have already outgrown? Put a price tag on it, and put it in the pile.

Whose opinion about how you are doing in your life do you no longer want or need? Find something that carries memories of these opinions, and ready it for release.

Who told you what you could and could not do with your life?

What beliefs did you grow up with that you do not want to carry on into the future?

What things have you done that have hurt you or others that you don't need to do anymore? Into the pile. It's all right if you feel some sadness now. These things you are letting go have been with you a long, long time.

How might things be different for you now?

Finish selecting items for your garage sale. See how light you feel? You can let go of old expectations, demands, and judgments. The past is not binding. It does not own you. You are your own person. You may not understand why this disappointment happened to you, the role it has played in your life. But consider this possibility, that the pain you have felt may not be about what's wrong with you—but about what's right. Release everything that no longer serves you and, increasingly, you will be left with what is essential and true for you.

67

Let Your Curiosity Lend You Courage

*I*n the early 1900s, a North American man named Ishi—the last Native American of his tribe—made a momentous decision. After living alone for some time, having watched his entire tribe succumb one by one to the ravenous appetites of the coyotes and wolves of Northern California, he suddenly appeared in Oroville, California, one day at dawn. Not knowing what to think of this strange naked man, the people of Oroville quickly clothed him and put him in jail. When the Bureau of Indian Affairs was contacted, Ishi's story hit the San Francisco dailies. Among those reading about Ishi was the anthropologist Alfred Kroeber, who brought Ishi to San Francisco; there, he was wined and dined by society, studied and entertained. He lived out his days in this strange new world remarkably at peace with himself and his fate.

The key to Ishi's resilience seemed to those who knew him to be his infectious curiosity. He had an openness, a willingness to try new things and ways of being, that was greater than any of the fear he may have been feeling. One oft-told story that illustrates Ishi's open stance in life goes back to that moment when he was first taken to the Oroville train station. As the train pulled into the station, Ishi quietly took refuge behind a cottonwood tree alongside the platform. His traveling companions beckoned to him, and together they boarded the train. Some time later, Kroeber and Ishi discussed that day. Ishi told Kroeber that he and his tribe had been aware of the train all his life, but that they had all assumed it to be a demon that ate people. They had watched it bellowing and smoking, and had seen people swallowed up within it never to emerge again. Kroeber listened to Ishi, wonder flooding over him. At last, he asked, "How did you have the courage to just get on the train if you thought it was a demon?" Ishi answered, "My life has taught me to be more curious than afraid."

When Ishi left the wilds and ventured onto the streets of Oroville, he had no guarantees that things would work out as well as they did. But he knew that he could not put things back in his life the way they used to be. He understood that there is no going back in life—only moving forward.

The time has come for you to let go of the fantasy that you can get things back just the way they were, as well. Regardless of how you and others count your losses, the truth is that you are changed as a result of what has happened. You cannot go back to the way things were—or that you hoped they could be—not only because the universe is in a constant state of change, but also because you are now a different person than you once were. You cannot know for certain the greatness of the future for which you are being prepared: the depths of compassion and understanding that are being carved by your sorrow; the vitality that gathers in secret pools behind the dam of old hopes and memories; the adventures that await you. Your inner spirit builds upon itself in anticipation of that final drop that will pour over the side and into your future. You do not even need to be conscious that this is happening in you. But even if you are not aware that this is going on, you cannot stop the life within you that is pressing forward.

Is there something you can do to help? Simply this. Be curious. Your curiosity will be the source of your courage.

Sacred Space

*"Do what you are doing now, suffer what you are
suffering now; to do this with holiness,
nothing need be changed but your hearts."*

—*J. P.* DE *C*AUSSADE

*O*ut of the depths you had not previously known wells up fresh courage. When you allow your disappointments to loosen your grip on the illusion of control, you leave behind ordinary definitions of success and failure. But know this: The cost is great. For by taking a leap of faith into sacred space, you expose yourself to the appearance of foolishness or weakness. If you have will enough to persist, you will discover that you are part of a whole, far greater than whatever private disappointment you have suffered. The diminishment of personal needs and desires before the urge for unity with the divine becomes not a means to an end, but the end itself.

68

Place Your Wager on Meaning

*"Even if one wagers one's life on ultimate
meaninglessness, that is no less a gamble."*

—W. PAUL JONES

One spring morning, I awoke from a disturbing dream with a horrible question formulating in my mind. There had been a series of upsetting occasions in the week preceding, in which I had felt called upon to give more of myself to my friends and situations than I was likely to receive in return. As I prepared to greet the day, I was unaccountably swept with an overwhelming sense of self-pity for all the sacrifices I've made in the name of love. Had my generosity, my charity, my reaching out to others merely made me weak—easy to take advantage of?

And then, as I sank deeper and deeper into a familiar hole I've been in too often before, I realized that my emotions had dug a hole so painfully deep, they'd exposed the terrible question that now sat heavily upon my chest, begging for a response: *Do I really believe that there exists for me and the universe a loving presence—or not?*

To reply in the negative would fully justify my sinking deeper into despair. If this is a dog-eat-dog world, I should, indeed, be watching out primarily for my own welfare. It was toward this possibility that all rational evidence pointed. I could easily answer "no." I do not believe the universe is loving.

On the other hand, I've learned from experience that whatever it might cost me, the only way up and out of this abyss would be to somehow find a "yes." Feeling the darkness closing in on me, I set my thoughts and even my feelings aside and leaped for "yes" as if it were a rope thrown to me from the depths of the mystery.

For regardless of how great the circumstantial evidence to the contrary, there is no alternative but to take the leap of faith that life has purpose, that self-sacrifice has meaning, that the divine calls to us for some greater purpose than we may ever be able to grasp fully. This, in fact, is the very essence of what I am experiencing when I refer to God. God is the transformed experience of being alive that causes us to transcend our self-interest in order to take the risk of believing that it is worthwhile to love others, to sacrifice for others, even knowing that in doing so, one becomes vulnerable, exposes oneself to pain and the potential for disappointment.

William James equates the leap to "yes" to the novice who, climbing a mountain for the first time in the Alps, finds himself in a situation in which the only escape is a terrifying leap across an abyss. Having had no experience with such a leap in the past, he has no basis upon which to assess his ability to survive the effort.

But he notes that hope and confidence will put him in a better frame of mind to succeed than would fear and mistrust. James writes:

> Believe, and you shall be right, for you shall save yourself; doubt, and you shall be right, for you shall perish. The only difference is that to believe is greatly to your advantage.

By leaping to "yes," you imbue your life with the possibility of meaning and purpose, even at the huge cost of defying reason and logic, even if it means exposing yourself to the appearance of weakness or foolishness. And finally, even if you must acknowledge the terrifying possibility that you may, in the end, have been mistaken.

69

Dip Your Toes in Mystic Waters

When you allow your disappointments to loosen your grip on the illusion of control, you leave behind ordinary definitions of success and failure. Out of depths you had not previously known wells up fresh courage. But even as you feel yourself being pulled toward renewed life, beware! For the cost is great. There will be times when you will feel as if you have been directed to march off the edge of a cliff, with only the endless void of the infinite to break your fall. Will it? If you are always sure that everything will turn out just the way you hope, then you are still clinging to the edge. The order you envision is quite simply not the order of the divine. To be fully alive is to rise and fall on the ever-changing tides of dread and awe. When you become certain, you fall. When you are cast out, you are found. Only when you become willing to embrace the whole range of human experience do you remove the impediments that separate you from connection to the divine.

This, then, is sacred space, the realm of the true mystic: not the illusion of tamed order, delivering you peace and love in reward for your obedience. But rather, creation out of chaos, the terror of plummeting through deep mystery, wrestling with your own embarrassing finitude. And then, impossibly, there are those rare, sublime moments when you experience the in-breaking of the divine. As mystic philosopher Charles Kingsley writes:

> When I walk the fields, I am oppressed now and then with an innate feeling that everything I see has a meaning, if I could but understand it. And this feeling of being surrounded with truths which I cannot grasp amounts to indescribable awe sometimes . . .

In these moments, you have a sense that you are part of a whole, far greater than whatever private disappointment you have suffered. The diminishment of personal needs and desires before the urge for unity with the universe is not a means to an end, but the end itself.

Once you have tasted such an awareness, even if but for a moment, you can begin to trust that there is meaning in your existence that transcends the ups and downs that fill your everyday life. For the spiritually gifted, it becomes more and more possible to set aside your primary concerns for safety and comfort to pay greater attention to the forces greater than but including yourself that are luring you forward. The truth is that you do not always know where you are heading, but you are content to be in free fall within the heart of the divine.

That you do not feel this way consistently is not a sign of personal failure. To reside in a constant state of oneness with the divine is the hallmark of the saint. While you may aspire to perfection, it is spiritually prudent to avoid erring on the side of excessive optimism. In the meanwhile, we find ourselves as spiritual beings in a constant wavering, first soaring and then descending. At the peak, we feel whole and connected. In the valley, we despair of ever again raising our heads above the mud. Yet there exists always the possibility that the divine will seek us out, in whatever state we may find ourselves.

Such moments of unity can happen to you regardless of the circumstances of your life at any given time. Even if you do not live permanently in such a state of perfect unity, once you have experienced the in-breaking of the divine, your life begins to pivot around this new, higher center. You know what true joy is and what is possible for you. It's not that you give up your everyday life, envisioning goals, carrying out plans, celebrating or mourning your results, but the drama of your circumstances is now played out against an infinite backdrop of all-encompassing love and mystery.

"God is not always silent, and man is not always blind," writes Rabbi Heschel. "There are moments in which . . . heaven and earth kiss each other."

70

Pull in Your Oars

In the mid-eighties, having added a second child on top of my eighty-hour workweeks, I knew that the various pieces of my life were being held together by cheap glue. I had invested long days and nights denying my own inner life, needs, and values in favor of pursuing the American dream. Once I attained my goal—having built a nationally respected public-relations agency—then I would be happy. But the thought was dawning on me that if I kept up the frantic, self-denying pace much longer, I would not be around to see that day. I realized I needed some time in my life to think about things. Time for my family. Time for myself.

I also needed to get in shape. Rowing was the answer. So there I was, one cool, misty morning, having undergone the recreational rower's training program, ready to take my first solo cruise onto the San Francisco Bay.

The thing is, it's not so easy to shift gears from the fast lane to quiet time. This morning, while typical, had already drained me. Somehow, my son's pants hadn't gotten washed over the weekend and he needed me to run them quickly through the washer and dryer by 7:00 A.M. My infant daughter and I were late getting out the door and nearly missed the daycare center's morning walk. My briefcase, stuffed with press releases that needed editing, waited for me on the front seat of my car, next to the suit I would be changing into in a little more than an hour.

But as I stepped into the sleek, high-tech craft, I vowed to put all that aside and get the revitalization I so sorely deserved. This was to be the beginning of the recovery of my life in earnest. On the bay, surrounded by gaily darting seagulls, I would row my spirit back to life. I cast off from the dock, the whole bay open to me. I could go anywhere. I was free. I could row back toward my home in Mill Valley. Or I could head out toward San Francisco, glimmering across the bay like the Emerald City. Then, there was the route that would take me past the houseboats to the foot of the Golden Gate Bridge. As the sun struck the bridge, it seemed to light up from within. I knew that I had been shown my direction. I would row out to the bridge and when I reached my goal, I would experience the peace I knew I deserved.

And so it was that I applied my strength to the task of rowing. Pull, lift, pull, lift. I remembered my instructor's directions as we had practiced during our series of training sessions. Pull, lift, pull, lift. I closed my eyes in ecstasy, knowing that in just a few moments, I would be leaving the houseboats behind and making my way to the bridge. Such pleasure! Such freedom!

I opened my eyes. Something was wrong. After long minutes of rowing, I was no closer to the houseboats than I'd been when I started. In fact, I may have even been farther away. I dug my oars into the water again, this time keeping my eyes wide open. Again, the boat did not budge. Then, as a bug on a leaf floated hastily past me, headed in the wrong direction, I realized the terrible truth. I was rowing against the tide. Couldn't I do anything right? There, before me, shimmering at the foot of the Golden Gate Bridge in the light of the new day, lay the promise of peace, perspective, and revitalization. And here and now, just as in my everyday life, my strength, my will, my training and technique, even my good intentions, were quite simply not good enough. I pulled up my oars and bent my head down into my arms, sobbing about the injustice of life. I mourned my own inadequate efforts to crack the secret code. I railed against my destiny. I railed against myself. And then finally, exhausted by the blinding emotion that had engulfed my inadequacies, I gave up. I would row back to the dock. Turn in my oars. And forget once and for all about my puny efforts to find meaning in my life.

But as I sat up, the dripping paddles resting on my legs, I realized that something was happening. The boat was moving. It was moving fast. It was moving effortlessly. The current had taken hold of it and was sweeping me around a hidden bend of the shore, toward a destination I had never noticed before. I neither helped nor hindered the boat's intention as it rapidly rounded the corner, slowed its pace, and finally ceased its motion. I looked about me, amazed. Somehow, I had found my way into a sparkling lagoon, the surface smooth as glass. Around me were bright green weeping willows, swaying gently in the warming breezes of the morning. For the first time in many years, I felt my heart deeply come to rest. I had not made this magical destination happen. Even as I had given up, pulled my paddles from the bay, and cried out in pain and hopelessness, my destiny had been moving me forward. And not just to the goal I had set, but to an experience far greater than I had ever envisioned for myself. I wept again, but this time in gratitude. As the hour came to an end, I effortlessly made my way back to the dock.

My son's pants would again need washing. There would be days when we would miss the daycare center's morning walk and find ourselves cruising the streets of San Francisco looking for the renegade battery of strollers. But rarely would I forget that there are forces greater than ourselves at work in our lives at all times. At those particular moments when all seems lost, we can always pull up the paddles and see where the current takes us.

71

Provide Shade

According to Chinese tradition, Lao-tzu's disciples were traveling through a forest one day where hundreds of trees had been cleared. In the center was one huge tree with hundreds of branches. Wood-cutters rested in its shade.

The disciples asked the woodcutters why the tree had been left standing.

"Because it is absolutely useless. The bark is so tough, it breaks our saws. And even if we are able to chop off a piece, the smoke it makes when burned stings our eyes."

When the disciples reported this conversation to Lao-tzu, he laughed.

"Be like this tree. Be absolutely useless. If you become useful, somebody will come along and make a chair out of you. Be like this tree and you will be left alone to grow big and full, and thousands of people will come to rest under your shade."

72

Think of Yourself as Experientially Gifted

*M*ysteries that initiate growth, compassion, and an expanded perception of the truth are being revealed to you now for reasons beyond your current comprehension. The setback you have suffered is the vehicle through which your greater purpose will be encountered.

Everyone knows the story of Joseph, the favored son of Jacob, who received a fabulous multicolored coat as a gift from his father. His brothers, jealous of his preferred status, stripped him of his coat and threw him into a pit to die. Brother Judah, relenting, came up with an alternative. "Come, let us sell him to the Ishmaelites." And so, Joseph was sold into slavery for twenty pieces of silver.

The Ishmaelites took Joseph with them to Egypt. Once in Egypt, keeping his wits through the highs and lows of fate, Joseph soon found his way into the court of the pharaoh himself. By interpreting the pharaoh's dreams, Joseph was able to prepare the country to withstand seven years of famine. In the midst of the famine, none other than Joseph's own brothers came to him, begging for food. So grand was Joseph, they did not recognize their own brother. When at last he revealed his identity to them, they were frightened and ashamed. They wept, fell down before him, and said, "We are here as your slaves." But Joseph said to them, "Do not be afraid! . . . Even though you intended to do harm to me, God intended it for good."

The pain you are experiencing is at this very moment expanding your capacity to embrace a fuller understanding of what it means to be fully alive.

No matter what harm others have intended for you, yet may God turn it for good.

73

Sit Alone in a Sacred Place

"Let me seek the gift of silence and poverty and
solitude, where everything I touch is turned
into prayer . . ."

—THOMAS MERTON

*H*ave you ever been in a sanctuary after hours, lights turned low, nobody but you sitting alone in the silence of sacred space?

The chatter in your brain quiets down and in this sacred realm—the moment beyond thought—there are no longer contradictions, opinions, or preferences.

You sit in solitude, and yet you are not lonely.

The darkened air settles about you, embracing you with comfort, expecting nothing in return.

And then, when all is perfectly still, a voice whispers to you:

"Will you let me love you?"

74

Trust the Impulse to Pray More Than the Prayer Itself

The maggid of Mezeritch was a storyteller, one of many who traveled from village to village bringing holy stories to life for the people of his time.

While the maggid was known for his devotion to God, he saw the injustice of the world around him: good people who suffered unfairly, bad people who prospered despite their evil deeds. And so it was that in the secret depths of his heart, he challenged God.

One day, as the maggid of Mezeritch prepared to speak, he heard a voice from on high saying that because he had challenged God, he would be denied access to heaven.

The maggid fell to his knees, overcome with joy. From now on, having been denied the rewards of goodness, he could be certain to serve God for God's own sake and not for any advantage to himself.

When you pray, there is a moment of perfection . . . a moment when you have truly made yourself known to the infinite. When is this moment? It is in the impulse to pray: the movement within your heart that turns to the divine; the pure moment of hope before you attempt to give shape to the yearnings of your soul in the form of words. What you think you want is always so much less than what you are truly yearning for. You are always more than your self-centered concerns. This infinite yearning is the prayer that is always heard, the prayer that is always answered.

75

Choose Your Wishes Wisely

Sometimes you wonder why others—who seem to be so much less deserving than you—get exactly what they want. You think you see people with flawed integrity succeeding, buying new cars, getting their pictures on the cover of *Time* magazine.

When you see individuals with selfish aspirations succeed, what you are in truth witnessing is the laying of the groundwork for their moment of reckoning. It may take time, and it may not be readily apparent to the outside observer, but it is inevitable. People who are willing to cut integrity's corner to succeed can often seem to gain the short-term advantage. Clever strategies can dazzle the marketplace. People loan them their power, some swept up through their own greed or naïveté, others joining in like sharks at the spoil. But people who put their personal desires ahead of the common good do not have a center that will hold over time.

The *I Ching* explains: "Where the community of interest ceases, the holding together ceases also, and the closest friendship often changes into hate. Only when a bond is based on what is right, on steadfastness, will it remain so firm that it triumphs over everything."

The ancient Chinese philosophy teaches us by asking us to observe the swamp plant, which grows fabulously tall overnight. Nearby, a tiny acorn—with great effort—sends up one tender shoot. Which plant, over time, contains the greatest potential? Come back tomorrow morning and you will see that the swamp plant is dead, withered, and fallen. And the acorn? It is continuing to do its quiet inner work, persevering day in and out to fulfill its destiny for greatness.

Life gives us many opportunities to develop spiritual muscle. When you judge yourself by others' external manifestations of success, you may be tempted to make your wishes unwisely.

Ask first for an inner life, rich with the courage of goodness. If you must judge yourself, set your standard by the quality of your aspirations and choose your wishes wisely.

76

Wake Up Singing

*E*very day of my young life, I awoke to the sound of my father's voice singing favorite tunes from Broadway musicals. No matter what challenges or disappointments had come home with him the previous day from work, no matter how great the insanity of the morning news, Dad sang.

The rest of us—taking it pretty much for granted as quite simply the way things always were and always would be in our house and in the world—went about our tasks: getting dressed, eating breakfast, gathering schoolbooks. We mumbled and grumbled as we rushed about preparing for the demands of the day, but we did so awash in the upbeat music of my father's voice. Each day was new and full of hope. Regardless of the challenges he personally faced, he created an environment for us each morning that was stable and whole. In fact, I now realize that what I got to experience every morning of my childhood was a sense of the holy.

It is no accident, perhaps, that twenty-five years ago, I married a man who also has music in his soul. There is music every night in our house. After dinner, Dan takes out his guitar and provides our evening hours with the background weavings of his soulful blues, jazz, and rock and roll. This is how Dan nurtures his soul and how he, too, weaves a fabric of holiness for our family life.

But as years, experience, and circumstances have rounded the corners of my innocence, I know that I cannot rely on any other individual's connection to spirit to embrace me fully. I can put a tape of my dad's singing on the recorder and put down my books to tune in to Dan's music, but I have realized that the sacred task of aligning myself with the goodness of creation is fundamentally my own responsibility. By building routines and order into my everyday life, I provide opportunities to open myself to higher dimensions. I don't always have access to the awe, dread, and wonder I know is possible for me, but through routines, I at least make myself available on a regular basis to the advances of the divine. Whether I feel like it or not, I journal, I walk, I read special books, I pray, I congregate. Every afternoon, as our family returns home, one by one, I remind myself how grateful I am to have each one of these special people in my life. When the spirit is with me, I celebrate. When the spirit is absent, I mourn. But regardless of my mood, or my results, the invitation to unity is always deep in my heart, weaving its divine connections with or without my conscious assent.

Through my father's songs, I grew up immersed in a sense of the orderliness of the universe—a sacred, optimistic center that could be bruised but not ultimately destroyed by any of the ups and downs of our ordinary lives. This was how my family prayed. This is how I aspire to live my life. Not a life filled with prayer, but life lived as prayer.

77

Watch the Sun Rise

When was the last time you really thought about the sun? How often have you enjoyed the light and warmth of its presence without stopping to think how far beyond our comprehension is this life-giving orb? Day after day, as you mourn your losses, the sun rises to fill the plants that will feed you with the energy to grow. The sun returns, morning upon morning, drying the flooded plains, moving the wind to caress, dance, or wrestle with you as you wait for the bus or pick up the newspaper. The sun asks nothing of you and yet it makes your life possible.

When was the last time you really thought about water? How often have you quenched your thirst without stopping to think of the miracle of molecules, invisible to the eye, combining to make liquid with which to sustain your life? Daily, you drink it. You bathe in it. Your disappointments come and go, some minor, some life-threatening, and through it all, you imbibe of the water of life with nary a thought.

When was the last time you really thought about the stars? The sky? The wild animals? The trees? If you were to but for one moment unveil your eyes and see all that you have been given, you would be engulfed with awestruck love of the universe.

You have your setbacks in life. Of course you do. There are things you want. Opportunities you've missed. But remember that when disappointment strips you of safety and comfort, the veil between you and the mystery is thin, indeed. When your pain is greatest, your investment in the illusions becomes most transparent. So little separates you from the luminous essence of true existence. Take advantage of this precious moment to look beyond the disarray of your human constructions and to experience the abundance of loving miracles that surround you always.

> You never enjoy the world aright till the sea itself floweth in your veins, till you are clothed with the heavens and crowned with the stars. . . . Till you are more present in the hemisphere considering the glories and the beauties there, than in your own house; till you remember how lately you were made, and how wonderful it was when you came into it.
>
> —THOMAS TRAHERNE

STAGE VIII

A New Center

"The secret is to be able to want one thing, to seek
one thing, to organize the resources of one's
life around a single end; and slowly, surely,
the life becomes one with that end."

—HOWARD THURMAN

As long as you are fully alive, you do not leap into the abyss once and then it's over. The truth is that the spiritual life is an existence that takes place in its entirety over the edge of mystery. If you hope to aspire to greatness of spirit, you must stay vigilant to the potential inherent in every moment. The present is always free and full of possibilities. It is up to you to choose that which will be best for you. Divine love urges you toward the greatest good, but does not force you. By heeding the impulse for the good that is present in any given moment, you contribute to the creation of a different and better future than would otherwise have occurred. The best outcome, given the circumstances, is always possible.

78

Go Fishing

Chinese tradition relates the story of Prince Wen Wang, who encountered an old man fishing. The story of the old man's life was carved deeply into the lines in his face, a lifetime filled with many joys and many sorrows. Prince Wen Wang watched in awe as the old man sat still, his line cast deep into the water. But his fishing was not what we think of as fishing, for it was apparent to the prince that the old man did not fish in order to catch fish, but solely to delight in the joy of fishing.

The thought occurred to Wen Wang that he must employ this old man in the administration of his government.

Many of us aspire to rise above the ups and downs of daily life:

our disappointments, our achievements, our desires. But this fisherman, all alone on the riverbank, had not risen above life. Rather, he had gracefully allowed the weight of his many years to strip his life to its barest essentials. We think we need so many things to make us happy, to give our lives meaning. We strive to become great, to stay young, to make our mark, to fulfill our promise. But if we are fortunate enough to live long and fully, we will understand how much of what we think we needed to be happy can be done without.

Having already sacrificed all her worldly attachments, at the age of sixty-six, Ryo-Nen, a Zen nun famed for her great beauty, made one last renunciation in this, her final poem:

> Sixty-six times have these eyes beheld
> the changing scenes of autumn.
> I have said enough about moonlight,
> Ask me no more.
> Only listen to the voice of pines and cedars,
> when no wind stirs.

Let life's losses help you strip away the superficial illusions, and you, too, will be gifted with a glimpse of what is real.

As John B. Cobb Jr. and David Ray Griffin write:

> To be responsible . . . is to share in the divine adventure in the world. Although the outcome is never assured, and although it entails the sacrifice of many past

forms of enjoyment, in itself it is joyful. The one who experiences the joy of this participation in the divine life hopes urgently for success, but accepts the risk that the only reward may be in the joy, itself.

79

Grab Your Flashlight

Joseph Campbell, in conversation with Michael Toms of *New Dimensions Radio*, shared his favorite quote from *La Queste del Sainte Graal*, the story of King Arthur's quest for the Holy Grail. In this episode, King Arthur's knights were seated at his table, but Arthur would not let the meal be served until an adventure had occurred. Sure enough, the Grail appeared to them, carried by angelic powers, veiled by cloth. Then, abruptly, it disappeared. Arthur's nephew Gawain proposed that the knights pursue the Grail in order to see it unveiled. And so off they went.

Campbell's favorite lines were these: "They thought it would be a disgrace to go forth in a group. Each entered the forest that he had chosen where there was no path and where it was darkest."

Campbell continued, "Now if there's a way or a path, it's someone else's way . . . What is unknown is the fulfillment of your own unique life, the likes of which has never existed on the earth. And you are the only one who can do it. People can give you clues how to fall down and how to stand up, but when to fall and when to stand, and when you are falling, and when you are standing, this only you can know."

When I first embarked on my spiritual journey, I believed that the goal was to achieve inner peace and stability. In order to attain this objective, I knew that I would need to be willing to let go of the status quo and leap into the void. Floating painfully through the dark night, I held on to my faith that I would someday, sooner or later, return to the safety of the shore—there to rest in the warm glow of peace forever.

While it is true that there are moments when I know that my soul is at home in the world, when the universe seems luminous with never-ending peace and joy, it is also true that I have discovered something I had not anticipated. The truth I have encountered on my own journey is this: So long as you are fully alive, you do not just leap into the abyss once and then it's over. The truth is that the spiritual life is an existence that takes place in its entirety over the edge. If you hope, as do I, to aspire to a greatness of spirit, there can be no safety in your choices. You must pay heed to your heart above all, discovering just how stringent a taskmaster one's spirit can be.

In *Leaves of Grass*, Walt Whitman describes the experience of life over the edge.

O to confront night, storms, hunger, ridicule,
      accidents, rebuffs, as the trees and animals do . . .
Dear Camerado! I confess I have urged you onward
      with me, and still urge you, without the least
      idea of what is our destination,
Or whether we shall be victorious, or utterly
      quell'd and defeated.

When moments of peace and faith come, they are such gifts—to be treasured as memories of the past and hope for what is yet possible. But they must not be clung to in the present, for too easily do they transform into pale imitations of themselves. Functioning nicely enough, going about your tasks efficiently, sacrificing your passion in order to win the praise of strangers. Quietly thumbing through your dreams: There is a great writer, a world traveler, an inspired romantic. But you dare not take them out to put them to the test. Keep your mouth shut to avoid rocking the boat. Stay in destructive relationships rather than demanding the respect you deserve. A single, failed try is not worth one thousand good illusions. Treading through your days, keeping an even keel through an ocean of low-grade blues.

Rather, spirit urges you to release again and again aspects of the status quo that are deadening to your spirit. You must be willing to listen to your heart, take risks, and come to stand for something greater than yourself. If you, too, are willing to let your greatness unfold, there is only one way that does not involve falling into the void. That is to climb down into it. Grab your flashlight and begin exploring. Questioning the meaning of life? Your higher purpose?

Go deeper. Go to the one place where it is easiest to let go of old ways of knowing that have not, cannot, and will not take you where you want to go. This is, I propose, the true understanding of what it means to fulfill your human potential.

Sounds daunting? Joseph Campbell offers this advice: "When the world seems to be falling apart, stick to your own trajectory, hang on to your own ideals and find kindred spirits. That's the rule of life."

80

You Never Awaken to the Same Day Twice

*E*verything is in constant motion, every moment arising out of all that has preceded it. While the past culminates in each present moment, the past does not wholly determine the future because in the present moment, you are free to make choices introducing completely new elements into the mix.

Present, too, in every moment is the tendency for good to prevail. You have within you intuition and wisdom that can be counted upon to provide you with the opportunity to actualize the best possibility available to you in every situation, "best" meaning that choice most in keeping with divine love.

Because you are free, however, you do not automatically respond to the impulse for good. You can reject, ignore, or block the reception of it in favor of any of the myriad possibilities that freedom makes available to you. Divine love urges you toward the greatest good possible, but does not force you. If your freedom is real, then so is your potential to make poor choices resulting in suffering and pain.

"Increasing the freedom of the creatures was a risky business on God's part. But it was a necessary risk, if there was to be the chance for greatness," write John B. Cobb Jr. and David Ray Griffin.

What is the deciding factor that turns one toward or away from the greatest good? It is your intention to do what is right and best that shifts the odds for the greatest possible success in your favor. That is the essential element that can always be trusted to act upon the past to create anew.

You are free and the future is uncharted. If you but intend to do what is best in the present moment, the odds for the greatest good possible will be with you.

81

Take a Stand

"The world consists of power struggles between competing values. The resolution of the power struggles will determine the very makeup of the universe . . ."

—LARRY GRAHAM

*I*t is possible that you have done all that is within your power to make peace with the disappointment you have suffered, and the role you played in it. And yet, your unrest persists.

There comes the time when you need to ask if the upset from which you attempt to flee is none other than the voice of the divine, calling you to action.

Oh, no, you demur. You regret your anger and your resentment. Spiritual discipline requires you to learn to forgive easily, and at all costs to put harmony over discord.

Nonsense, says Confucius, who was once asked by his disciple, "What would you say if all the people of the village like a person?"

Confucius replied, "That is not enough."

"What would you say if all the people of the village dislike a person?"

"That is not enough," Confucius answered, explaining, "It is better when the good people of the village like him, and the bad people of the village dislike him."

We cry out for peace and comfort, but it is time for us to confront the darker truth that spiritual maturity may march us, often against our desires, to the brink of righteous anger. We must, when we realize we have no choice in the matter, be willing to take a stand for what we know is right. In her novel *Voice in the House*, Pearl Buck writes:

> Against the tyranny of the inferior man, the superior man also has the right to be free . . . For good people to feel pain and to take action against the inferior is the hope of humanity.

How much of the disappointment that remains in you, resisting your attempts at resolution, confession, and positive affirmation, has not been caused by your own shortcomings, but by society's failures? Could this be the long-awaited time for you to turn your anger into action? Has your diffuse depression been none other than the denial of your prophetic urge, begging you to give it expression?

William James writes:

> Much of what we call evil . . . can so often be con-
> verted into a bracing and tonic good by a simple change
> of the sufferer's inner attitude from one of fear to one of
> fight; its sting so often departs and turns into relish
> when, after vainly seeking to shun it, we agree to face
> about and bear it . . .

You have been on the run, chased by the fear of your misfortune. Now you must stop running and take a stand. You must be
willing to honor your intention to engage in the struggle, no matter how it may turn out. You must confront the fact that you may
not be able to save the world single-handedly, that you may make
enemies, that you may cause yourself pain, and yet you must do
what you can. You matter. What happened to you matters. You
have an important job to do. Only you can do it.

Start an organization, write a letter in protest, hire a lawyer,
join with others of like mind, vote, protest, tell the truth out loud,
let your voice be heard.

If this is the occasion to which you must arise, hear this: The
very makeup of the universe is depending upon you.

82

The Better Question Is Not How to Become Happy, but Rather What Is Being Asked of You

You cannot go for enlightenment directly. Peace and happiness cannot be attained by frontal attack. You cannot achieve them in the same way you set out to climb a mountain or wage a battle.

When you cease asking *What can I do to be at peace,* and begin inquiring *How do I do what's right,* only then do you become a candidate for unity with the divine. Peace and happiness are the by-products that derive spontaneously from the living of such a life.

Jane Steger, in *Leaves From a Secret Journal,* says that for a long time she resisted surrendering to her higher purpose because she was so sure that God would ask her to do something so overwhelming that her courage would fail her in the undertaking. Struggling with her anxiety, she was finally able to set aside her concerns and look to what was being asked of her. To her astonishment, what God needed of her at that moment was to clean out the drawers of her bureau and keep them neat and orderly.

If you look squarely into the heart of your disappointment, you will discern the truth of what you are, at this moment, being called to do. Of course, you prefer that surrendering to your highest purpose might require nothing more of you than cleaning your drawers. But if you hope to achieve true peace and happiness, you must begin by telling the truth about what your heart is asking of you.

83

Wrestle With Angels

"One can choose harmony over intensity, thus reverting to a more trivial existence in order to avert discord."

—JOHN B. COBB JR.

Jacob, son of Isaac, sought to win divine blessing, but his efforts were flawed. He cheated his brother Esau of his birthright, then left home to make his fortune. But when midlife came, he began to long for the one thing all his clever manipulations had failed to bring him: reconciliation. He set out for his childhood home, willing to do whatever it would take to rectify his past. Jacob knew what he wanted, but along the way—on the banks of the Jabbok River—he was met by an agent of God who engaged him in a life-or-death struggle. All night long, Jacob wrestled the angel for his life. When morning dawned, wounded though he was by his struggle, Jacob at last received God's true, though hard-won, blessing from the angel. Jacob had been willing to take a stand for what he wanted—to put his very life on the line for it. He was even willing to take God on in hand-to-hand combat, if necessary. And in the end, he got what he wanted.

Life does not want you to tiptoe around your spirit, fearful of stepping on toes, overstepping bounds. No, divine love wants you vigorous and alive, willing to put your life on the line for what you have been called to do, even if that means struggling with the very essence of the divine. Sometimes you are called to struggle for others. Sometimes you are called to struggle for yourself.

Twelve African American men were accused and jailed unjustly in Elaine, Arkansas. Visiting them in their cell, Ida B. Wells-Barnett spoke these words:

> I have been listening to you for nearly two hours. You have talked and sung and prayed about dying, and forgiving your enemies, and of feeling sure you are going to be received in the New Jerusalem . . . But why don't you pray to live and ask to be freed? . . . Quit talking about dying . . . Pray to live and believe you are going to get out.

You must not settle for premature resolution when what you are truly being asked to do is to fight for what is right. Your life is precious, your existence meaningful. Don't be too quick to accept your fate.

However it is you are being called, trust that when you respond to the impulses placed within you by the divine—no matter how impudent or disloyal to God you fear yourself to be—you are creating the environment in which miracles are most likely to transpire.

Higher-Quality Problems

"God requires a faithful fulfillment of the merest trifle given us to do, rather than the most ardent aspiration to things to which we are not called."

—Saint Francis de Sales

Ironically, when you give up your resistance to human limitations, only then will you have your full potential available to create and to build. To make this transition, you need only understand that as long as you are always going to have problems, you might as well begin to have problems worthy of you.

84

Seek a Shaman

*"If you attempt to obtain by force something for
which the time is not yet ripe, you'll injure
yourself by expending your strength
prematurely."*

— THE *I* CHING

There is so much that we hope to accomplish, and sometimes
things take so much longer than we would wish. Last summer, Dan
and I were frustrated with the pace of our overall spiritual progress.
We each thought we should have more to show for all the effort
we'd expended over the years. Happily, our twenty-fifth anniversary
came in the midst of our impatience, giving us several weeks' worth
of distraction as we pursued our long-anticipated plan to journey
to the Navajo reservation Canyon de Chelle.

For years we had hoped to spend time in the shadows of the
canyon's ancient cliffs, covered with many centuries of inhabitants'

cave paintings. But additionally, Dan and I shared a secret ambition. Perhaps in the canyon, we would encounter a genuine shaman—someone of mystical depth who could help us understand why there so often seemed to be such a time lag between our willingness to heed the behests of our hearts and the harvesting of our results.

As we neared the canyon, our senses went on alert. Just how does one go about seeking a real shaman? The only way into the canyon, it turned out, was on a guided tour. Surely we could find a secret route in. In the town outside the gates, we went to Laundromats and read the bulletin boards, hoping to find an advertisement for shamanic guidance. There were used motorbikes and weight-loss powders, but no shamans. We read the local newspapers and scrutinized every wrinkled face. We were determined to have some kind of spiritual adventure. Nothing happened.

After several hours, we sadly surrendered our quest for the extraordinary, deigning at last to stand in line with all the other tourists, to buy our half-day ticket to the Canyon de Chelle bus tour. We wearily handed our tickets to the tour guide, a middle-aged Navajo who had grown up in the Canyon de Chelle, and then we settled back to salvage whatever we could by taking in the magnificent scenery. The guide, who doubled as driver, pointed out all the sights to us, as he must do several times a day. Here were ancient dwellings, carved into the canyon wall; there were tan-and-red-etched hieroglyphics of deer and mystic dancers. The guide spoke softly, and we strained to hear him over the choppy noise of rubber tires rolling over sand and rock on the canyon floor. After a long, bumpy hour, we pulled up to a rest stop. A dozen canyon residents were there to greet us, blankets laden with jewelry and hand-painted pots sparkling tantalizingly in the sun. Our bus-mates swarmed, but Dan and I noticed our guide off in the shadows, plucking a small wildflower, carefully wrapping it in tissue, and putting it in his shirt pocket.

Curious, we approached him to ask about the plant.

"I have been looking for this flower for some time," he explained. "Collecting plants is part of my training."

"Your training?" we asked. What could gathering plants possibly have to do with leading canyon tours?

"Yes. My training as a medicine man."

Medicine man! We had found our shaman after all—driving the tour bus at Canyon de Chelle. Did he know how to heal, then—not only physical, but spiritual things? We eagerly awaited his response.

"Not until I'm in my sixties," he answered. "We can't begin our serious training until we are sixty. Until then, I help out as I am asked, gathering plants and such."

Sixty! For a moment, the three of us middle-aged seekers stood facing one another, quietly appreciating all that we endured, in various states of surrender and impatience, while awaiting the fulfillment of our respective callings. So even among the Navajos, one is not born a shaman, but must wait until the age of sixty before developing the depth of life experience, the character, and the spirit necessary to support such a destiny. And in the meanwhile? What do shamans do before they are old enough to practice their ancient art? One drives the tour bus, gathering plants on the side.

It would be twenty years before the medicine man in training who stood before us could respond to our souls' yearnings with official words of wisdom and transformation. But right here, right now, the Canyon de Chelle tour guide provided us with the answer we'd been searching for. He taught us how to wait.

85

Clean Up the Mess

The villager went to the rabbi to complain about his cramped house. It felt old and stuffy, and when he was inside it, he felt stifled by the atmosphere. The rabbi had some advice. Buy a chicken and put it near the fireplace. The villager, thinking that this must be a magical solution, took the rabbi's advice. The chicken, however, soon began shedding his feathers and scattering his cornmeal all over the house. The room felt more cramped than ever. The villager went back to see the rabbi.

"Your solution is not working," the villager said.

"Buy a goat and let it live beside the chicken," the rabbi replied.

The villager did as he was instructed. But soon the goat was chasing the chicken around the house, knocking over the furniture. Before long, there was no place untouched by the unruly creatures. The villager returned to the rabbi.

"I've put the chicken and the goat in the house near the fireplace," he explained, "but things have only gotten worse."

The rabbi responded, "Bring your cow inside, as well."

For several weeks, the villager lived amid the chaos, waiting for the miracle he expected to occur. The house only got messier. Finally he could stand it no longer. He hurried back to the rabbi, totally distressed by the situation.

"I can wait no longer," the villager cried. "Please, Rabbi, you must help me! I did as you say, bringing the chicken, the goat, and the cow into the house. What should I do now?"

"Take them out of your house," he replied.

The villager rushed to comply. He put the chicken into its coop, tied the goat and the cow to stakes in the yard, and cleaned the mess out of his house. As evening fell, the villager looked about his house. It was so roomy and full of space. He sighed deeply and lit a candle in gratitude for the great miracle that had transpired.

86

Choose Problems That Are
Worthy of You

$\mathcal{A}$ parable from ancient India tells the story of a farmer whose crop of wheat suffered first from locusts, then from floods. Although his family had enough to eat, they could not get ahead. The farmer turned to the gods and begged for one perfect season.

"Please send me plenty of sunshine and just the right amount of rain, no pests, and a gentle breeze."

The farmer got exactly what he asked for, watching his new crop of beautiful wheat grow tall. He fell to his knees to offer his gratitude, but in the distance he heard his wife cry out. She had opened the husks and found them empty. Without resistance, the wheat had failed to produce its seed. Still on his knees, the farmer continued, "But next year, send me just enough troubles to make my wheat strong."

You think you don't want problems. But if it were possible, it would not be the best thing for you. Like the wheat, you, too, need something to push against to make your character strong. Surrender to the imperfection of the human condition, and you can stop wasting your energy repressing negative possibilities. You will have your full potential available to you to create and to build. To make this transition, you need only understand that as long as you are always going to have problems, you might as well begin to have problems worthy of you. Take a risk, go for what you really want, come to stand for something.

Yesterday, I bumped into Sam, an acquaintance I hadn't seen for some time. The last time we'd spoken, he had just been passed over for a big promotion. Needless to say, he was disappointed and upset.

A year had passed, but when I saw Sam again he had that same troubled expression on his face.

Was he still reeling from his bitter loss?

"Not at all," he replied. "Several months ago, I finally got up the courage to hand in my resignation."

"That's terrific," I said. "You made the decision to look for something better for you. But why, then, do you still look so concerned?"

"The conflict is killing me!" Sam answered. "You see, I've received several great job offers and I'm not sure which to take."

87

Make a Two-Hundred-Year Plan

"The meaning of awe is to realize that life takes place under wide horizons, horizons that range beyond the span of an individual life or even the life of a nation, a generation, or an era."

—Rabbi Abraham Joshua Heschel

The most joyful person I know is a college professor who left his secure position to take on the problem of homelessness in one of our country's biggest cities. The man is not young—and the task he took on was huge. At a time when many of his peers were settling down to collect on a lifetime of goodwill and academic merit, he was selling off his worldly goods and going to live as a resident manager in an inner-city shelter.

"You can't be serious!" I overheard one of his young students say to him. "How much can one person accomplish given the time you have left?"

Rather than reacting to the students' innocent rudeness with a rebuke, the professor sighed deeply and replied, "I know my time is short and the task is huge. But what you don't understand is that what I'm doing is just the first part of a two-hundred-year plan."

For a long time, you have struggled to discern the true purpose of your life. You have worried that you have blown your opportunity for greatness. You fear that you have wasted your life and that there is so little time left. You have been burned out, sometimes by your efforts to inspire the world for the sake of humanity, more often by trying to get the world to do what you want it to do to make your life less painful.

But now you have arrived at the present moment. Worn out from wrestling with yourself and your life though you may be, yet is there a secret voice whispering to you that you are already making your contribution. You contribute every time you even make the attempt to heed your higher impulses, regardless of the results you have to show for yourself at this moment in time, however foolishly you have passed your time until now, however small but sincere your effort. Upon this foundation, a better future than would otherwise have come to be is being built.

Olive Schreiner writes of many of us in *Dreams of the Hunter:*

> I have sought; for long years, I have laboured; but I have not found her [truth] . . . Now my strength is gone. Where I lie down worn out, other men will stand,

young and fresh. By the stairs that I have built, they will mount. They will never know the name of the man who made them. At the clumsy work they will laugh; when the stones roll they will curse me. But they will mount, and on my work; they will climb, and by my stair.

88

Blaze a Secret Route

$\mathcal{M}$aimonides, the twelfth-century Jewish sage, recognized the existence of thirty-two secret routes to unity with God. While these routes were open to all, they would surely have been most familiar to the tzaddikim.

Who are the tzaddikim? Tradition teaches that they are righteous people, "freed from the restraints of fame," for whose sake God keeps the world in existence. There are thirty-six such individuals in each generation, walking this secret path. They may include the humble village shoemaker of my great-grandmother's generation, who never let it be known outside the tight-knit circle of his own family that he was one of the greatest scholars of his time. He worked at his cobbler's bench all day and studied all night. According to tradition, it was only after his death that his brilliant writings, which had been hidden under his mattress, came to light.

Or perhaps it is the schoolteacher, who takes money out of his own pocket to give to his poor students so that they may ride home on the bus rather than walk through the muddy streets on cold winter nights.

Do you know a tzaddik? *Could you be one yourself?* We must all try to live our lives as if we are. But heed this warning: The more sure you may be that you are, the less likely it is to be the case. This path is so secret that even the true tzaddik does not know that he or she is walking it.

89

Be Specialized—Not Special

When you make the decision to fulfill your higher purpose, the greatest temptation is to feel special about yourself. You realize that having courageously responded to your calling, you have become better than you used to be. And so, it is the easiest thing to slip into the assumption that you are better than other people, as well.

Early in his career, Marshall found that he had a natural talent for keeping audiences enthralled. A motivational speaker, he began his career sharing stories about how he had overcome the hardships to which he was born. Among those things that he had to overcome was a rare, gradually debilitating, but nonfatal illness, for which there was yet no cure. Courageous and optimistic when others would have given up, he had defied the odds by living three full, happy decades, with no sign of slowing down. Marshall realized that he had a special gift to share with his audiences and so he began to seek and accept invitations to tell his story. So full of life was Marshall that despite his lack of training—and more than a touch of nervousness—his story overflowed his heart and bathed his audiences with inspiration.

Before long, Marshall began getting as many engagements to speak as he could handle. He expected that as he lost his nervousness, his speaking would become more and more effective, but the opposite began to occur. Rather than receiving unanimous raves on his feedback forms, his statistics began to slip.

Then, one day, flying home after a speech that drew a mixed reception, Marshall found himself seated next to a woman whom he recognized as having been in that day's audience. Realizing that she might be a bit intimidated by him, Marshall made a special effort to appear relaxed and friendly. The two began to chat, as he generously shared himself with her. Having established a warm level of rapport, he finally got up the nerve to ask her how she had rated his speech.

"I thought it was outstanding," she replied. "In fact, I'm sure it changed my life—and it may, in fact, change yours, as well. You see, the illness that you suffer from—I am on a team of medical researchers who are on the verge of developing a cure. There's just one detail we still had to work out, and for months, we've been blocked. But while you were talking, something you said triggered something in me. I now know what we need to do."

As Marshall's career had advanced, he had begun to think of himself as having a special calling. While he was not aware of his own subtle arrogance, somehow he had placed himself as separate and above the very people he had set out to serve. Naturally, when he found himself seated next to one of his audience members, he assumed that his special role would be taken for granted. But with her confession, his whole life turned upside down. Not only was there now hope for a reversal of his disabilities, but he found himself reconnected to the source of his original inspiration.

In short, he realized that each of them—both he and his travel companion—had, not a special calling, but a specialized one. His job was to inspire her. Her job was to create a cure. And if each of them had a specialized calling, then wasn't it possible that each and every person in his audiences—and in his life—also had a specialized calling? Not better, not worse—simply specialized: the mailman, the garbage collector, the physicist, the president? Not special—specialized.

Now when Marshall speaks, his numbers are way back up. Through his travel companion, he connected up with an experimental program, testing the research team's breakthrough cure. And ever on the alert lest success and happiness once again sweep him away, Marshall no longer thinks of himself as special, but specialized.

90

Do Your Utmost

"Through all the world there goes one long cry from the heart of the artist: 'Give me leave to do my utmost!'"

—ISAK DINESEN, BABETTE'S FEAST

Sheila was trained as a modern dancer. While her parents warned that there was no future in the arts, dance was her calling and so she responded. Throughout her teens and twenties, she performed with a troupe on the East Coast, getting by with little income but a spirit full of life and love. But when she reached thirty years of age, modern dance on the wane, the troupe disbanded and Sheila went back to her childhood home for what she thought was to be a temporary visit. When she arrived, it became clear to her that her aged and ailing parents needed her assistance. "Just for a while," she told herself. She packed away her leotard and dancing shoes into a box in the attic, and took a job in the local bookstore.

Because her spirit had been so well nurtured for so long, Sheila took her change of fortune with grace and dignity. She tended her parents lovingly, and proved herself to be adept at serving customers enthusiastically. She was promoted once, then twice, to the position of bookstore manager. She made several close friends. Often she thought longingly of her career in modern dance, but she could find no way to make it back to the East Coast. Deep down, she always thought of herself as a dancer, but as each year passed, her return became less and less likely. Not only was modern dance a thousand miles away, but her body had begun to age seriously. And yet she was never bitter.

At last her parents passed away, first her mother, then soon after, her father. She was left with the little house and enough money to make her way back east. After the last mourner left the house, she went up to the attic, took down the box, and put on the leotard and dancing shoes.

She danced as she had never danced before, knowing that as she leaped and turned, she yet had it in her to give her life her utmost. She danced all night, until the light of dawn announced the beginning of a new day. Quietly, she took off her leotard and dancing slippers, placed them back into the box in the attic, and got dressed for work.

Beyond Resilience

"*Don't blame God for having created the tiger, but give him thanks for not having given the tiger wings.*"

—Amharic Tribal Saying

The art of resilience is not about learning to negotiate with the universe to draw from its wells only that which we would prefer for ourselves. The true purpose of spiritual training is to faithfully remove any of the obstacles that separate you from divine love. You must search your soul for hidden resistance, pockets of arrogance and selfishness. At the same time, you must open yourself to the unbounded joy of the universe, and stand before the mystery of divine love in awe and reverence. If you are courageous enough to embark on the path of resilience, it is time to relinquish the expectation that you will get things back the way they were. You must be willing to be profoundly changed.

91

Allow Yourself to Be Changed

The American Heritage Dictionary defines *resilience* as "the ability to recover quickly from illness, change, or misfortune to retain its original shape."

But is this always true?

What about those times when recovery will require more of us than simply snapping back into our original shape—those times when the transformation will be deep and painful and profound?

Misfortune strips away our illusions that we can be smart enough, good enough, lucky enough to get through life untouched. Spiritual growth is not about learning how to obtain only that which we would prefer for ourselves. The true purpose of spiritual training is to unclog the channels that connect us to divine love.

Mystic philosopher Aldous Huxley explains that to do so, we must take on the task of engaging with the circumstances of our lives—no matter how trivial or threatening—without malice, greed, or voluntary ignorance. Rather, we must rise to the challenges that arise moment by moment with love, courage, and understanding. We must search our souls for hidden resistance, pockets of arrogance and selfishness.

> Because its objectives are not limited, because for the lover of God, every moment is a moment of crisis, spiritual training is incomparably more difficult and searching than military training. There are many good soldiers, but few saints.

92

Carve Something Out of Wood

Philosopher and mystic Chuang Tzu tells the story of Ch'ing, the chief carpenter of ancient China, who set himself to the task of carving a music stand out of wood. So superlative was Ch'ing's work that upon finishing, all those of the imperial court who saw it exclaimed that it must be of supernatural origin.

"What secret is there in your art?" asked Prince Lu.

"No secret, Your Highness," replied Ch'ing. "And yet there is something. When I am about to make such a stand, I quiet my mind and guard against any diminution of my spirit.

"Three days in this condition, and I become oblivious of any reward to be gained.

"Five days, and I forget about any fame to be acquired.

"Seven days, and I become unconscious of my physical body.

"Then, when there is no thought of the court present in my mind, my skill becomes concentrated, and all disturbing elements from without are gone. Then I enter some mountain forest, searching for a suitable tree. When I find the right tree, I can see the stand in my mind's eye. Then I set to work.

"Beyond that, there is nothing. I bring my own native capacity into relation with that of the wood. What was suspected to be of supernatural execution in my work is due solely to this."

93

Teach the Lump in Your Throat to Sing

You have deep inside of you your own special art—yearnings to create, to communicate, to bring to life—those deepest expressions of yourself that are unique to you. If unexpressed, they sit like a lump in your throat, begging you to loosen your grasp on more practical considerations in order to sing them to life. You owe it to life to bring them forth. The unfinished song in the bottom drawer of your desk; the poetry that hides in your journal pages, waiting to be sculpted into final form; the box of paints that calls you from the utility shelf in the garage; the unopened application to go study what your heart is begging of you.

What are the reasons you give for leaving these things untouched? You are too busy to get to them, you say. You have more useful things to tend to. After you've cleaned the house, gotten the promotion, saved enough to retire on . . . And in the meanwhile, your soul whispers to you that it's dying of thirst. But you are too responsible taking care of everything and everybody else to hear.

Hear now, lest you face the grim regret that Olive Schreiner warns of in *From Man to Man:*

> . . . When he is dying, they gather round him, the things he might have incarnated and given life to—and would not. All that might have lived, and now must never live forever, look at him with their large reproachful eyes—his own dead visions, reproaching him; "Was it worth it? All the sense of duty you satisfied, the sense of necessity you labored under; should you not have violated it and given us birth?"

But it is not too late for you. There is some way you can give expression to these things, even in the context of your present life and responsibilities. You can add your deepest expression into the kaleidoscope of duties, dashes of shimmering gold and red to make the whole of your life into a work of art. Don't worry any more about whether it's useful, what will come of it, will it be good enough to sell, will others appreciate or understand it. This is not about earning a living from it, turning your soul into some useful commodity that others may package and sell. This is about you giving life to your deepest impulses, engaging with the mystery without needing to know how or why. Trusting.

You have enough to mourn in your life without needing to take on the burden of unnecessary regrets. Foolishly leap from your practical concerns and let the lump in your throat issue forth its song of life.

94

Skate On

When she was but ten years old, Ekaterina Gordeeva met her partner in life. For fourteen years, they skated together, winning two Olympic gold medals and four world championships. But he was more than her partner on the ice. Sergei Grinkov became her husband and father of their daughter. Their relationship was profound and it was glorious. Skating through life in a symphony of love and spirit, they graced us with their beauty.

And then, one day, while skating on the ice in Lake Placid, New York, Sergei placed his familiar hands around Ekaterina's waist one last time and then, suddenly, fell to the ice. Hours later, he had died of massive heart failure. With the final beat of his heart, their life together was over. And gone, too, at age twenty-four, was

Gordeeva's career as the world's top woman pairs skater. She knew she could never skate with anyone else.

Several months passed. The skating world, bereaved with their terrible loss, planned a tribute to Sergei. Baiul, Yamaguchi, Witt, Boitano, Petrenko—they all offered to take to the ice in "A Celebration of Life." Would Ekaterina honor them with her presence?

She responded that she would come. She would be present. And she would skate.

Ekaterina dedicated her brilliant performance to all those "who have to start all over again, stand up from their knees." As the music began, she stood alone in the middle of the ice. She hesitated, hands covering her eyes in disbelief. She looked longingly at the stands, as if searching for somebody who wasn't there. She raised her fists in rage. She dropped to her knees. Then, lifted by the strains of Mahler's Fifth Symphony, she soared off the ice on wings of steel.

95

Set Your Dry Bones Dancing

"The hand of the Lord . . . set me down in the
middle of a valley; it was full of bones . . .
they were very dry . . . suddenly there was a
noise, a rattling, and the bones came together,
bone to its bone . . ."

—Ezekiel 37

When I was younger, I played a secret game with myself. I would look at very old faces, drawn and tired, or plump and wrinkled, and try to imagine the person within as a teenager or child. Occasionally it was surprisingly easy, plump cheeks peeking out over fluffy pale blue baby blankets topped by whispery tufts of hair from a bald head. More often, I could not pull back the layers of time to see the firm red lips of the ingenue I knew—from the stories and pictures—who had flirted and preened and danced across the stage of youth with the best of them in her time.

But I do not play this game anymore. I do not need to. For by looking in my own mirror, revealed to me under the harsh glare of fluorescent lights, I have learned to read the many ages we have been by studying the history of my own face. I no longer see the very old as other. Instead, I drink deeply from the vast well of time, thinking about the future as well as the past. I look for evidence of the life well-lived. I want to learn.

Tucked into the pages of my journal is a yellowing clipping from the *Los Angeles Times*. The column, on the occasion of New Year's 1995, is by journalist Jack Smith, made all the more poignant by his death not long after. In this column, Jack reviews his year. Prominent in it were the neurologist who diagnosed his Parkinson's disease, the dermatologist who diagnosed his skin cancer, the orthopedist who put a cast on his broken wrist, the podiatrist who attended his broken ankle, the audiologist who fitted him with hearing aids. There's his wheelchair, his cane, his physical therapist, and his wife, who prepares his pills and insulin shots four times a day and turns the newspaper pages for him, "impossible to do with one hand."

"She also dresses and undresses me because I can't handle the subtle movements required. Also, I can't button a shirt or get into a coat or tie my shoelaces. It takes about as long to dress me as it must have taken to dress Queen Victoria. She also takes me to the bathroom."

Just prior to Christmas, Jack's two daughters-in-law took him to Bullock's Pasadena to buy a present for his wife. No sooner had they entered the store than he saw a gray-green pantsuit with a mandarin collar. He knew immediately that he had found the perfect gift. His wife wore it on Christmas night.

"She looked beautiful," Jack writes. "I haven't lost my touch."

So what did Jack Smith resolve for that New Year's? What could such a man as Jack have to hope for from the year to come?

"As for New Year's resolutions, I have only the same old one. Try to keep on living and see what happens next."

To have lost so much, and yet to feel so much gratitude. To have every reason in the world to have given up, and yet to continue to feed the flame of life. To eschew self-pity in favor of submitting his love, painful although it must have been, to words. Jack, can my dry bones learn to dance, too?

96

Jump at the Sun

*"Mama exhorted her children at every opportunity
to 'jump at de sun.' We might not land on
the sun, but at least we would get off the
ground."*

—ZORA NEAL HURSTON

*I*n the secret recesses of your heart, there is something you would love to do. But you have allowed the circumstances of your life to dim your light. You have listened to the voices of reason and of fear, allowing yourself to sacrifice your passion for safety and for acceptance.

But the voice that sounded alone for so long whispers to you still: Take the risk. Do something fresh, new, unexpected, daring—something that challenges those who have laid claim to you. Feel the adrenaline pulse; let your heart race!

97

Find Someone to Tickle You

When life is looking particularly dark, and you feel yourself to be especially concerned, discipline yourself to ask of yourself what I discovered some time ago to be the most important question: *Is there any chance I am taking things a bit too seriously right now?*

98

Cultivate a Taste for the Bittersweet

*"The soul . . . judges itself by choosing, in accord
with the character formed during its life on
earth, what sort of an afterlife it shall have."*

—ALDOUS HUXLEY ON THE
TIBETAN BOOK OF THE DEAD

The old woman stood before the angel, so many tears streaming down her face that she could not read the letters on the gate. While she had always tried to live a good life, the sorrow that consumed her sent a shiver of fear down her spine. At last, trembling in fear, she managed to ask the angel her question.

"Am I at the gate of heaven—or of hell?" she whispered.

"Tell me first," the angel replied. "Why are you crying?"

The old woman stopped to think, and into her mind flooded images of all that she had left behind. Not only the old man, with whom she'd spent fifty years, but the memories of a lifetime full of simple joys and unavoidable losses. Her parents, young and full of life, pushing her proudly through the streets of their neighborhood in a brand-new stroller. Childhood friends building castles in the sand, blown to dust by the churning wheels of time. High-school proms, college, their wedding night. Then there were her babies— first steps, names in school programs, graduations, leaving home for the last time, children no more. Along the way, there were new houses, new cities, new jobs—some left out of choice, some not. There was falling down and starting over again. And then, too, there was the gradual loss of her physical vitality and ultimately her own death.

Witnessing all, the angel finally replied, "Only one who has loved so greatly can feel such great pain. You stand here before the gate to heaven or to hell. And so it is before I answer your question that you must answer one for me. Have you been blessed or have you been cursed?"

So surprised was she by the angel's words that her eyes suddenly cleared. Had she been blessed or had she been cursed? For many moments, she reviewed her life, pondering the angel's question.

"If it was a curse," she finally declared, "I would give none of it back."

With that, her fear departed, leaving in its wake only the bittersweet song of her love. Had she given her life her very best? She no longer needed to read the word above the gate to determine her destiny. The angel took her hand and together they walked through the gate. Upon each of their cheeks lay a single salty tear.

99

Try Again

*I*t is sometimes painful to pick up the pieces and go on living.

It takes so much courage to confront the limits of my power and yet be willing to try again.

The more I yearn to serve, the more aware of my own shortcomings I have become.

So often, I wonder if I am heeding my true purpose calling me, or if my yearnings are merely a projection of my own fear or desire.

When things go badly for me, I am so afraid that I have taken matters into my own hands and forgotten to ask what's right.

When things start to turn out for me, I am so quick to forget that this is about my serving the greater good—not about my own glory.

I fall short of my own ideals over and over.

Yet, despite the certainty of my unworthiness, I feel spirit urging me to venture forth again.

So, God, I ask you to use me, anyway.
Take my fears and use me, anyway.
Take my failures and use me, anyway.
Take my arrogance and use me, anyway.
Take my greed and use me, anyway.
Take my guilt and use me, anyway.
Take my confusion and use me, anyway.
Take my regret and use me, anyway.

I offer all of myself to you.
Use me to serve many or few,
In pain or in joy.
Use me as you will.

100

Make Your Life a Work of Art

Resilience is not about results. How wealthy are you? How successful is your marriage? How many promotions/degrees/honors have you earned?

When you judge your life by your results, working only to celebrate your achievements, you value only your products. Of course sometimes you can make it look good—like a piece of art hung on somebody's wall—but you will miss the point.

The secret to the art of resilience is this: Life is not about products—it's about process. Our souls are not the cold perfection of a cut diamond, but the tumultuous, organic stuff of creation! Struggle, repent, forgive, take risks, succeed and fail, feel remorse, feel gratitude, mourn, love, and celebrate: This is where the juice is.

Why waste your time mastering life's technology in an effort to get what you want when so much more is available to you than you'd ever dreamed possible?

The art of resilience does not conclude with a specific result. Rather, it asks something much greater of you: that you make your whole life a work of art. The uncertainties of life, the pain and problems, let them become woven into the fabric of your being—alongside the joys and the triumphs. This is life's promise to you, not that you will always get what you think you want. But that you can become great enough to embrace it all. Live your life fully—there is no easier way. Make your life a work of art—it is enough.

The Ten Stages of Resilience

STAGE I: POINT OF IMPACT

In the beginning, the pain is acute. Your tendency is to pull back—to avoid the suffering at all costs. But the emotions you are experiencing are not the obstacles to your healing. In fact, they are the very means of your deliverance. Your tears will wash away the illusions of what you once believed to be true but that you did not have strength to hold on to after all that has transpired. You will confront loss, humiliation, powerlessness, uncertainty, mortality. But you cannot rebuild a life structure stronger than it was, unless these bricks, too, are laid into the foundation of the human condition. At this point of your journey, the best thing to do is learn to be patient with your pain. As you do, you will discover that without having to do anything but feel, you are doing the important work of providing a more solid basis upon which a more authentic existence can be built.

STAGE II: TIME TO REGROUP

You fear you are alone. But it is the essence of divine love that is manifesting in your heart as the craving for resilience. The emotional pain you feel contains the seed of the answers you are seeking: wisdom beyond that which logic and rational thought could produce, resources you did not know you had. As the initial impact of what has happened to you recedes, you begin to find opportunities to nurture your spirit at the deepest levels. Cultivate within

yourself qualities of character, such as strength, faith, and persever-
ence; you will fortify yourself for the greater role you are being prepared to play in the world.

STAGE III: SIGNS OF SPRING

Everything is in a constant state of change. At this moment,
you may feel that winter has bared your branches. But neither you,
nor anyone else, can judge what is really going on with you by
looking only at your external manifestations. How reluctantly you
shed the vivid colors of autumn, now enriching the soil of your
roots. Beneath your naked limbs, new life is being readied to blossom forth. When you are fully alive, you are continually asked to
let go of what you have in order to prepare the way for new possibilities to come to you. Tend what is passing but put your energy
into what is birthing. As you do, you put forces in motion that will
bring to you new strength, courage, and opportunities.

STAGE IV: THE AUTHENTIC LIFE

True humility is the act of stripping away false notions about
yourself and the situation you face in order to deal with what is
real. When you have suffered a loss, it takes great strength to tell
the whole truth about yourself and the situation, resisting the urge
to select only that evidence that validates the least optimistic interpretation of circumstances. Now is the time to be simple. Don't let
yourself get swept up in other people's agendas for you, or your old
ideas of what your life ought to look like. Prepare to be surprised.

STAGE V: UNFINISHED BUSINESS

There comes a time when it's time to stop thinking and start doing. Now is the time to rectify any part you may have played in what has transpired: Get involved in the situation you've been avoiding; sacrifice your own comfort to right the wrongs. Your body and soul beg you to remove the blockages and let your spirit flow again. The very moment you begin making choices with integrity is the very moment that true healing begins. From that instant on, although external outcomes may continue to unfold as the consequence of what has been set in motion, inner failures are somehow rectified. Responding to the need deep in your soul, every step forward will be an occasion to rejoice.

STAGE VI: UNCHARTED TERRITORY

When you have forgiven others, mourned your losses, salvaged the best possible outcome, you have done enough about the past. Now is the time to leave the charted waters of your misfortune, setting out through treacherous seas to ports unknown. While it is true that you can influence your fate, you cannot control it. No matter how hard you try, how smart or wise you are, your life will spin out of your control from time to time. There are no guarantees. The risk is great. But if you hope to master the art of resilience, quite simply, you have no choice. You must allow yourself to respond to the urge calling you beyond the familiar and into the unexplored territory of fresh vision where the questions are as important as the answers.

STAGE VII: SACRED SPACE

Out of depths you had not previously known wells up fresh courage. When you allow your disappointments to loosen your grip on the illusion of control, you leave behind ordinary definitions of success and failure. But know this: The cost is great. For by taking a leap of faith into sacred space, you expose yourself to the appearance of weakness or foolishness. If you have courage enough to persist, you will discover that you are part of a whole, far greater than whatever private disappointment you have suffered. The diminishment of personal needs and desires before the urge for unity with the divine becomes not a means to an end, but the end, itself.

STAGE VIII: A NEW CENTER

As long as you are fully alive, you do not leap into the abyss once, and then it's over. The truth is that the spiritual life is an existence that takes place in its entirety over the edge. If you hope to aspire to greatness of spirit, you must stay vigilant to the potential inherent in every moment. The present is always free and full of possibilities. It is up to you to choose that which will be best for you. Divine love persuades you toward the greatest good possible, but does not force you. By heeding the impulse for goodness that is present in any given moment, you contribute to the creation of a better future than would otherwise have occurred.

STAGE IX: HIGHER-QUALITY PROBLEMS

Ironically, when you give up your resistance to human limitation, only then will you have your full potential available to you to create and to build. To make this transition, you need only understand that as long as you are always going to have problems, you might as well begin to have problems worthy of you.

STAGE X: BEYOND RESILIENCE

Spiritual growth is not about learning to negotiate with the universe to draw from its wells only that which we would prefer for ourselves. The true purpose of spiritual training is to faithfully remove any of the obstacles that separate you from divine love. You must search your soul for hidden resistance, pockets of arrogance and selfishness. At the same time, you must open yourself to the unbounded joy of the universe, and stand before the mystery of divine love in awe and reverence. If you are courageous enough to embark on the path of resilience, the first step is to relinquish the expectation that you will get things back the way they were. You must be willing to be profoundly changed. The deeper the channels pain carves into your soul, the greater the capacity for joy your soul can contain. Let yourself be used!

Sources

....

$\mathcal{A}$ number of the stories I share in this book are classics in their traditions. When a single author or source can be identified, I have done so in the body of the book. Otherwise, while crediting the tradition from which the story sprang, I have taken the liberty of telling my own version of the story. Other versions of many of the stories can be found in these valuable books.

Barry, William A. S. J. "Spiritual Direction," *Clinical Handbook of Pastoral Counseling*, vol. 1, edited by Robert J. Wicks, Richard D. Parsons, Donald Capps. New York: Integration Books, 1985.

Borysenko, Joan, Ph.D. *Pocketful of Miracles: Prayers, Meditations and Affirmations to Nurture Your Spirit Every Day of the Year*. New York: Warner Books, 1994.

Brammer, Lawrence. *How to Cope with Life Transitions: The Challenge of Personal Change*. New York: Hemisphere Publications, 1991.

Burns, David, M.D. *Feeling Good: The New Mood Therapy*. New York: Avon Books, 1980.

Chase's Annual Events. Chicago: Contemporary Books, 1992.

Chodron, Pema. *Start Where You Are: A Guide to Compassionate Living*. Boston: Shambhala, 1994.

Citron, Sterna. *Why the Baal Shem Tov Laughed: Fifty-two Stories about Our Great Chasidic Rabbis*. Northvale, New Jersey: Jason Aronson Inc., 1993.

Cobb, John B., Jr. and Griffin, David Ray. *Process Theology: An Introductory Exposition*. Philadelphia: The Westminster Press, 1976.

Doyle, Brendan. *Meditations with Julian of Norwich*. Santa Fe, New Mexico: Bear and Company, 1983.

Goodheart, Annette. *Healing our Grief With Laughter and Tears* (Video). Nashville: UMCom Productions, 1996.

Gratton, Carolyn. *The Art of Spiritual Guidance*. New York: Crossroad, 1995.

Heschel, Abraham Joshua. *I Asked for Wonder*, edited by Samuel H. Dresner. New York: Crossroad, 1983.

Heschel, Abraham Joshua. *A Passion for Truth*. New York: Farrar, Straus and Giroux, 1973.

Heschel, Abraham Joshua. *The Sabbath*. New York: Farrar, Straus and Young, Inc., 1951.

Huxley, Aldous. *The Perennial Philosophy*. New York: Harper and Brothers, 1945.

James, William. *The Varieties of Religious Experience: A Study in Human Nature*. Introduction by Reinhold Niebuhr. New York: Collier Books, 1961.

Janoff-Bulman, Ronnie. *Shattered Assumptions: Towards a New Psychology of Trauma*. Toronto: Maxwell MacMillan International, 1992.

Jones, W. Paul. *Trumpet at Full Moon: An Introduction to Christian Spirituality as Diverse Practice*. Louisville, Kentucky: Westminster/John Knox Press, 1992.

Kroeber, Theodora. *Ishi in Two Worlds*. Berkeley, California: University of California Press, 1969.

Larson, Bruce. *Living Beyond Our Fears: Discovering Life When You're Scared to Death*. San Francisco: Harper and Row, 1990.

Lubarsky, Sandra B., and Griffin, David Ray, eds. *Jewish Theology and Process Thought*. New York: State University of New York Press, 1987.

McNight, Reginald, ed. *Wisdom of the African World*. Novato, California: New World Library, 1996.

Merton, Thomas. *The Way of Chuang Tzu*. Boston: Shambhala, 1992.

Metzger, Bruce M., and Murphy, Roland E. *The New Oxford Annotated Bible*. New York: Oxford University Press, 1991.

Orsborn, Carol. *How Would Confucius Ask for a Raise?: One Hundred Enlightened Solutions for Tough Business Problems*. New York: Avon, 1994.

Orsborn, Carol. *Solved by Sunset: The Right-Brain Way to Resolve Whatever's Bothering You in One Day or Less.* New York: Crown, 1996.

Parry, Glenys. *Coping with Crises.* New York: Routledge, Chapman and Hall, 1990.

Rosten, Leo. *The Joys of Yinglish.* New York: McGraw-Hill, 1989.

Rupp, Joyce. *May I Have This Dance?,* Notre Dame, Indiana: Ave Maria Press, 1992.

Shak, Idries. *Tales of the Dervishes.* New York: E. P. Dutton, 1970.

Telushkin, Joseph. *Jewish Literacy.* New York: William Morrow, 1991.

Telushkin, Joseph. *Jewish Wisdom.* New York: William Morrow, 1994.

Thompson, Marjorie J. *Soul Feast.* Louisville, Kentucky: Westminster/John Knox, 1995.

Thurman, Howard. *Disciplines of the Spirit.* Richmond, Indiana: Friends United Press, 1963.

Townes, Emilie M., ed. *A Troubling in My Soul: Womanist Perspectives on Evil and Suffering.* Maryknoll, New York: Orbis Books, 1993.

Underhill, Evelyn. *Practical Mysticism.* New York: E. P. Dutton and Company, 1915.

Wieland-Burston, Joanne. *Chaos and Order in the World of the Psyche*. London: Routledge, 1992.

Wilhelm, Richard, and Cary F. Baynes. *The I Ching*. Foreword by Carl Jung. Princeton, New Jersey: Princeton University Press, 1950.

Wink, Walter. *Engaging the Powers*. Augsburg Fortress, 1992.

For Information

*I*f you would like to add your name to Carol Orsborn's mailing list, or to attend or start a regional discussion group based on her philosophy, please write to Inner Excellence Roundtable, P.O. Box 159061, Nashville, TN 37215. For speaking engagements and workshops, call 615-321-8890 or E-mail Carol at corsborn@aol.com.

About the Author

Carol Orsborn earned her Masters of Theological Studies degree from Vanderbilt University, where she teaches courses for both the Divinity School and the Owen Graduate School of Management Center for Leadership Development. Her previous books include *How Would Confucius Ask for a Raise?* and *Solved by Sunset.* She has led resilience workshops for major corporate clients around the country. She has appeared on *Oprah!* and the *Today* show. She lives in Nashville, Tennessee and can be reached at corsborn@aol.com.